KT-486-622

Coll. of Ripon & York St John
3 8025 00130749 8

STUDIES IN BRITISH ART

THE PAINTINGS OF
J. M. W. TURNER

Revised Edition

MARTIN BUTLIN and EVELYN JOLL

Plates

Published for The Paul Mellon Centre
for Studies in British Art and
The Tate Gallery by
YALE UNIVERSITY PRESS
NEW HAVEN AND LONDON · 1984

Designed by John Nicoll and set in Monophoto Ehrhardt

Text printed in Great Britain by
BAS Printers Limited, Over Wallop, Hampshire

Illustrations printed in Great Britain by
Westerham Press, Westerham, Kent

Library of Congress Cataloging in Publication Data

Butlin, Martin.
The paintings of J.M.W. Turner.
(Studies in British Art)
Bibliography: v. [1] p.
Includes indexes.
Contents: [1] Text—[2] Plates.
1. Turner, J.M.W. (Joseph Mallord William),
1775–1851—Catalogs. I. Turner, J.M.W. (Joseph
Mallord William), 1775–1851. II. Joll, Evelyn,
1925– . III. Paul Mellon Centre for Studies in
British Art. IV. Tate Gallery. V. Title. VI. Series.
ND497.T8A4 1984 759.2 84-40182
ISBN 0-300-03276-5 (set)
ISBN 0-300-03361-3 (pbk)

List of Plates

1. (Cat. 1) *Fishermen at Sea*, exh. 1796; $36 \times 48\frac{1}{8}$; Tate Gallery
2. (Cat. 2) *Moonlight, a Study at Millbank*, exh. 1797; $12\frac{3}{8} \times 15\frac{7}{8}$; Tate Gallery
3. (Cat. 3) After *Fishermen coming ashore at Sun Set ('the Mildmay Seapiece')*, exh. 1797; plate 40 from the *Liber Studiorum*, published February 1812; $7\frac{1}{8} \times 10\frac{3}{8}$
4. (Cat. 6) *Dunstanborough Castle*, exh. 1798; $36\frac{1}{4} \times 48\frac{1}{2}$; National Gallery of Victoria, Melbourne. Presented by the Duke of Westminster, 1888
5. (Cat. 7) *Buttermere Lake*, exh. 1798; $36\frac{1}{8} \times 48$; Tate Gallery
6. (Cat. 5) *Morning amongst the Coniston Fells*, exh. 1798; $48\frac{3}{8} \times 35\frac{5}{16}$; Tate Gallery
7. (Cat. 12) *Dolbadern Castle*, exh. 1800; $47 \times 35\frac{1}{2}$; Royal Academy of Arts
8. (Cat. 9) *Harlech Castle*, exh. 1799; $34\frac{1}{4} \times 47$; Yale Center for British Art, Paul Mellon Collection
9. (Cat. 11) *Kilgarran Castle*, exh. 1799; 36×48; National Trust, on loan to Wordsworth House, Cockermouth
10. (Cat. 13) *The Fifth Plague of Egypt*, exh. 1800; 49×72; Indianapolis Museum of Art. Gift in memory of Evan F. Lilly
11. (Cat. 14) *Dutch Boats in a Gale (the 'Bridgewater Seapiece')*, exh. 1801; $64 \times 87\frac{1}{2}$; Private Collection, England
12. (Cat. 16) *Fishermen upon a Lee-Shore, in Squally Weather*, exh. 1802; 36×48; Southampton Art Gallery
13. (Cat. 17) *The Tenth Plague of Egypt*, exh. 1802; $56\frac{1}{2} \times 93$; Tate Gallery
14. (Cat. 18) *Ships bearing up for Anchorage (the 'Egremont Seapiece')*, exh. 1802; 47×71; Petworth House
15. (Cat. 19) *Jason*, exh. 1802; $35\frac{1}{2} \times 47\frac{1}{8}$; Tate Gallery
16. (Cat. 19a) *Watermill and Stream*, *c.* 1791–2; $9\frac{3}{4} \times 11\frac{13}{16}$; British Museum
17. (Cat. 22) *Limekiln at Coalbrookdale*, *c.* 1797; $11\frac{3}{8} \times 15\frac{7}{8}$; Yale Center for British Art, Paul Mellon Collection
18. (Cat. 20) *Self-Portrait*, *c.* 1793; $20\frac{1}{2} \times 16\frac{1}{2}$; Indianapolis Museum of Art. Gift in memory of Mr and Mrs Hugo O. Pantzer by their children
19. (Cat. 25) *Self-Portrait*, *c.* 1798; $29\frac{1}{4} \times 23$; Tate Gallery
20. (Cat. 33) *Shipping by a Breakwater*, *c.* 1798; $11\frac{7}{8} \times 7\frac{5}{8}$; Tate Gallery
21. (Cat. 23) *Interior of a Romanesque Church*, *c.* 1795–1800; $24 \times 19\frac{3}{4}$; Tate Gallery
22. (Cat. 24) *Interior of a Gothic Church*, *c.* 1797; $10\frac{15}{16} \times 16$; Tate Gallery
23. (Cat. 28) *Caernarvon Castle*, *c.* 1798; $5\frac{13}{16} \times 9\frac{1}{16}$; Tate Gallery
24. (Cat. 26) *Plompton Rocks*, *c.* 1798; $48 \times 54\frac{1}{4}$; the Earl of Harewood
25. (Cat. 27) *Plompton Rocks*, *c.* 1798; $48 \times 54\frac{1}{4}$; the Earl of Harewood
26. (Cat. 29) *View in Wales*, *c.* 1799–1800; $22\frac{7}{8} \times 28\frac{5}{8}$; Tate Gallery
27. (Cat. 31) *View of a Town*, *c.* 1798; $9\frac{1}{2} \times 12\frac{3}{4}$; Tate Gallery
28. (Cat. 32) *Dunstanborough Castle*, *c.* 1798; $18\frac{1}{2} \times 26$; Dunedin Public Art Gallery
29. (Cat. 33a) *A Scene on the English Coast*, *c.* 1798; $9\frac{7}{8} \times 11\frac{15}{16}$; Phillips Collection, Washington, D.C.
30. (Cat. 34a) *A Dark Landscape with Trees and Mountains*, *c.* 1798–9; $12\frac{1}{4} \times 15\frac{1}{4}$; British Museum
31. (Cat. 35) *Wild Landscape with Figures, Sunset*, *c.* 1799–1800; $10\frac{5}{16} \times 15\frac{1}{4}$; British Museum
32. (Cat. 36) *Cilgerran Castle*, *c.* 1799; 22×27; The Viscount Allendale
33. (Cat. 37) *Cilgerran Castle*, *c.* 1798; $23\frac{3}{4} \times 29\frac{1}{4}$; The Leicestershire Museum and Art Gallery, Leicester
34. (Cat. 38) *Mountain Landscape with a Lake*, *c.* 1799–1800; $25\frac{1}{4} \times 38\frac{7}{8}$; Fitzwilliam Museum, Cambridge

35. (Cat. 39) *Landscape with Lake and Fallen Tree*, *c.* 1800?; $15\frac{3}{8} \times 23\frac{7}{8}$; Tate Gallery
36. (Cat. 40) *A Storm in the Mountains*, *c.* 1801–2; $9\frac{1}{2} \times 12$; Lady Kleinwort
37. (Cat. 41) *Tummel Bridge, Perthshire*, *c.* 1802–3; $11 \times 18\frac{1}{4}$; Yale Center for British Art, Paul Mellon Collection
38. (Cat. 42) *View on Clapham Common*, *c.* 1800–2; $12\frac{5}{8} \times 17\frac{7}{16}$; Tate Gallery
39. (Cat. 35c) *A Beech Wood*, *c.* 1799 or 1801; $6\frac{1}{2} \times 9\frac{1}{2}$; Fogg Art Museum, Cambridge, Mass.
40. (Cat. 35a) *A Beech Wood with Gipsies round a Camp Fire*, *c.* 1799 or 1801; $10\frac{3}{4} \times 7\frac{1}{2}$; Fitzwilliam Museum, Cambridge
41. (Cat. 35b) *A Beech Wood with Gipsies seated in the Middle Distance*, *c.* 1799 or 1801; $10\frac{3}{4} \times 7\frac{1}{2}$; Fitzwilliam Museum, Cambridge
42. (Cat. 35d) *Knockholt Park, Kent*, *c.* 1798 or 1801; $9\frac{1}{2} \times 6$; present whereabouts unknown (from old photograph)
43. (Cat. 35i) *'An Evening Effect'; Trees at Knockholt*, *c.* 1801; $9\frac{1}{2} \times 6\frac{1}{2}$; British Museum
44. (Cat. 35g) *Chevening Park*, *c.* 1801; $10\frac{3}{4} \times 14\frac{11}{16}$; British Museum
45. (Cat. 35h) *Chevening Park*, Kent, *c.* 1801; $10\frac{15}{16} \times 17\frac{7}{8}$; British Museum
46. (Cat. 35e) *The Kitchen of Wells's Cottage, Knockholt*, *c.* 1801; $10\frac{3}{4} \times 14\frac{3}{4}$; British Museum
47. (Cat. 35f) *Interior of a Cottage*, *c.* 1801; $10\frac{3}{4} \times 14\frac{1}{2}$; British Museum
48. (Cat. 35j) *An Armchair*, *c.* 1801; $8\frac{1}{2} \times 7\frac{1}{4}$; British Museum
49. (Cat. 150) *Venus and Adonis*, *c.* 1803–5; 59×47; Private Collection, South America
50. (Cat. 34) *Æneas and the Sibyl, Lake Avernus*, *c.* 1798; $30\frac{1}{8} \times 38\frac{3}{4}$; Tate Gallery
51. (Cat. 226) *Lake Avernus: Æneas and the Cumaean Sybil*, 1814–15; $28\frac{1}{4} \times 38\frac{1}{4}$; Yale Center for British Art, Paul Mellon Collection
52. (Cat. 43) *Diana and Callisto*, after Richard Wilson, *c.* 1796; $22\frac{1}{4} \times 36$; Tate Gallery
53. (Cat. 44) *Tivoli: Temple of the Sibyl and the Roman Campagna*, after Richard Wilson, *c.* 1798; 29×38; Tate Gallery
54. (Cat. 45) *Landscape with Windmill and Rainbow*, partly after Thomas Gainsborough, *c.* 1795–1800; $27\frac{3}{4} \times 35\frac{1}{2}$; Tate Gallery
55. (Cat. 47) *The Festival upon the Opening of the Vintage of Macon*, exh. 1803; $57\frac{1}{2} \times 93\frac{1}{2}$; by permission of Sheffield City Art Galleries
56. (Cat. 46) *Bonneville, Savoy, with Mont Blanc*, exh. 1803; 36×48; Newhouse Galleries, New York
57. (Cat. 124) *A View of the Castle of St Michael, near Bonneville, Savoy*, exh. 1812; $36\frac{1}{4} \times 48\frac{1}{2}$; courtesy, John G. Johnson Collection, Philadelphia
58. (Cat. 48) *Calais Pier*, exh. 1803; $67\frac{3}{4} \times 94\frac{1}{2}$; reproduced by courtesy of the Trustees, The National Gallery, London
59. (Cat. 50) *Châteaux de St. Michael, Bonneville, Savoy*, exh. 1803; 36×48; Yale Center for British Art, Paul Mellon Collection
60. (Cat. 49) *Holy Family*, exh. 1803; $40\frac{1}{4} \times 55\frac{3}{4}$; Tate Gallery
61. (Cat. 51) *Old Margate Pier*, exh. 1804?; $10\frac{7}{8} \times 16$; Ernest H. Gaskell, Esq.
62. (Cat. 52) *Boats carrying out Anchors and Cables to Dutch Men of War, in 1665*, exh. 1804; $40 \times 51\frac{1}{2}$; in the collection of the Corcoran Gallery of Art, Washington, D.C., Bequest of William A. Clark
63. (Cat. 53) *Narcissus and Echo*, exh. 1804; 34×46; Petworth House
64. (Cat. 54) *The Shipwreck*, exh. 1805; $67\frac{1}{8} \times 95\frac{1}{8}$; Tate Gallery
65. (Cat. 55) *The Deluge*, exh. 1805?; $56\frac{1}{4} \times 92\frac{3}{4}$; Tate Gallery
66. (Cat. 56) *The Destruction of Sodom*, exh. 1805?; $57\frac{1}{2} \times 93\frac{1}{2}$; Tate Gallery
67. (Cat. 57) *The Goddess of Discord in the Garden of the Hesperides*, exh. 1806; $61\frac{1}{8} \times 86$; Tate Gallery
68. (Cat. 58) *The Battle of Trafalgar, as seen from the Mizen Starboard Shrouds of the Victory*, exh. 1806 (reworked 1808); $67\frac{1}{4} \times 94$; Tate Gallery
69. (Cat. 59) *The Victory returning from Trafalgar*, exh. 1806?; $26\frac{3}{8} \times 39\frac{1}{2}$; Yale Center for British Art, Paul Mellon Collection
70. (Cat. 60) *Walton Bridges*, exh. 1806?; $36\frac{1}{2} \times 48\frac{3}{4}$; the Loyd Collection
71. (Cat. 63) *Walton Bridges*, exh. 1807?; $36\frac{1}{4} \times 48\frac{1}{8}$; National Gallery of Victoria, Melbourne. Felton Bequest, 1919–20
72. (Cat. 61) *Fall of the Rhine at Schaffhausen*, exh. 1806; 57×92; courtesy of Museum of Fine Arts, Boston. Purchased with bequest of Alice Marian Curtis and from Special Picture Fund
73. (Cat. 62) *Sheerness and the Isle of Sheppey, with the Junction of the Thames and Medway*, exh. 1807; $42\frac{3}{4} \times 56\frac{1}{2}$; National Gallery of Art, Washington D.C., Widener Collection
74. (Cat. 64) *The Thames near Windsor*, exh. 1807?; 35×47; Petworth House
75. (Cat. 65) *Newark Abbey on the Wey*, exh. 1807?; $36 \times 48\frac{1}{2}$; Yale Center for British Art, Paul Mellon Collection
76. (Cat. 66) *Cliveden on Thames*, exh. 1807?; $15\frac{1}{8} \times 23$; Tate Gallery
77. (Cat. 67) After *The Mouth of the Thames*, exh. 1807? Mezzotint by Sir Frank Short, R.A.
78. (Cat. 68) *A Country Blacksmith disputing upon the Price of Iron*, exh. 1807; $21\frac{5}{8} \times 30\frac{5}{8}$; Tate Gallery
79. (Cat. 69) *Sun Rising through Vapour: Fishermen cleaning and selling Fish*, exh. 1807; $53 \times 70\frac{1}{2}$; reproduced by courtesy of the Trustees, The National Gallery, London
80. (Cat. 70) *Union of the Thames and Isis*, exh. 1808; $35\frac{3}{4} \times 47\frac{3}{4}$; Tate Gallery
81. (Cat. 71) *The Thames at Eton*, exh. 1808; $23\frac{1}{2} \times 35\frac{1}{2}$; Petworth House
82. (Cat. 72) *Pope's Villa at Twickenham*, exh. 1808;

$36 \times 47\frac{1}{2}$; Trustees of the Walter Morrison Picture Settlement

83. (Cat. 73) *View of Richmond Hill and Bridge*, exh. 1808; 36×48; Tate Gallery
84. (Cat. 74) *Purfleet and the Essex Shore*, exh. 1808; 36×48; Private Collection, Belgium
85. (Cat. 75) *The Confluence of the Thames and the Medway*, exh. 1808; 35×47; Petworth House
86. (Cat. 76) *Sheerness as seen from the Nore*, exh. 1808; $41\frac{1}{2} \times 59$; the Loyd Collection
87. (Cat. 77) *The Forest of Bere*, exh. 1808; 35×47; Petworth House
88. (Cat. 78) *Margate*, exh. 1808; $35\frac{1}{2} \times 47\frac{1}{2}$; Petworth House
89. (Cat. 79) *A Subject from the Runic Superstitions* (*?*), exh. 1808?; $36\frac{1}{4} \times 48$; Tate Gallery
90. (Cat. 80) *Spithead: Boat's Crew recovering an Anchor*, exh. 1808; $67\frac{1}{2} \times 92\frac{5}{8}$; Tate Gallery
91. (Cat. 81) *The Unpaid Bill*, exh. 1808; $23\frac{3}{8} \times 31\frac{1}{2}$; Private Collection, U.S.A.
92. (Cat. 82) *Sketch of a Bank, with Gipsies*, exh. 1809?; $24\frac{1}{8} \times 33$; Tate Gallery
93. (Cat. 83) *The Quiet Ruin, Cattle in Water; a Sketch, Evening*, exh. 1809?; $24\frac{1}{8} \times 30\frac{1}{8}$; Tate Gallery
94. (Cat. 84) *River Scene with Cattle*, exh. 1809?; $50\frac{1}{2} \times 68\frac{1}{2}$; Tate Gallery
95. (Cat. 85) *Shoeburyness Fisherman hailing a Whitstable Hoy*, exh. 1809; 36×48; National Gallery of Canada, Ottawa
96. (Cat. 86) *Thomson's Æolian Harp*, exh. 1809; $65\frac{5}{8} \times 120\frac{1}{2}$; City Art Galleries, Manchester
97. (Cat. 87) *Fishing upon the Blythe-Sand, Tide setting in*, exh. 1809; 35×47; Tate Gallery
98. (Cat. 88) *Near the Thames' Lock, Windsor*, exh. 1809; $35 \times 46\frac{1}{2}$; Petworth House
99. (Cat. 89) *Ploughing up Turnips, near Slough*, exh. 1809; $40\frac{1}{8} \times 51\frac{1}{4}$; Tate Gallery
100. (Cat. 90) *Harvest Dinner, Kingston Bank*, exh. 1809; $35\frac{1}{2} \times 47\frac{5}{8}$; Tate Gallery
101. (Cat. 91) *Guardship at the Great Nore, Sheerness, &c.*, exh. 1809; 36×49; Private Collection, England
102. (Cat. 92) *Trout Fishing in the Dee*, exh. 1809; 36×48; Taft Museum, Cincinnati, Ohio
103. (Cat. 95) *The Sun rising through Vapour*, exh. 1809?; $27\frac{1}{2} \times 40$; the Barber Institute of Fine Arts, University of Birmingham
104. (Cat. 97) *London*, exh. 1809; $35\frac{1}{2} \times 47\frac{1}{4}$; Tate Gallery
105. (Cat. 100) *The Garreteer's Petition*, exh. 1809; $20\frac{7}{8} \times 30\frac{3}{4}$; Tate Gallery
106. (Cat. 98) *Tabley, the Seat of Sir J. F. Leicester, Bart.: Windy Day*, exh. 1809; $36 \times 47\frac{1}{2}$; Victoria University of Manchester
107. (Cat. 99) *Tabley, the Seat of Sir J. F. Leicester, Bart.: Calm Morning*, exh. 1809; 36×48; Petworth House
108. (Cat. 101) *Grand Junction Canal at Southall Mill*, exh. 1810; $36\frac{1}{4} \times 48$; Private Collection, London
109. (Cat. 102) *High Street, Oxford*, exh. 1810; $27 \times 39\frac{1}{2}$; the Loyd Collection
110. (Cat. 103) *Lake of Geneva, from Montreux, Chillion, &c.*, exh. 1810; $41\frac{1}{2} \times 65$; Los Angeles County Museum of Art, Adele S. Browning Memorial Collection. Donated by Mildred Browning Green and Judge Lucius Peyton Green
111. (Cat. 104) *Linlithgow Palace, Scotland*, exh. 1810; 36×48; Walker Art Gallery, Liverpool
112. (Cat. 105) *Fishmarket on the Sands—Hastings?*, exh. 1810; $35\frac{3}{4} \times 47\frac{1}{2}$; William Rockhill Nelson Gallery and Atkins Museum of Fine Arts, Kansas City
113. (Cat. 106) *Calder Bridge, Cumberland*, exh. 1810; 36×48; Professor Hamilton Emmons
114. (Cat. 107) *Dorchester Mead, Oxfordshire*, exh. 1810; $40 \times 51\frac{1}{4}$; Tate Gallery
115. (Cat. 108) *Cockermouth Castle*, exh. 1810; $23\frac{3}{4} \times 35\frac{1}{2}$; Petworth House
116. (Cat. 111) *Lowther Castle, Westmorland, the Seat of the Earl of Lonsdale: Evening*, exh. 1810; $35\frac{1}{2} \times 48$; Private Collection, England
117. (Cat. 112) *Lowther Castle, Westmorland, the Seat of the Earl of Lonsdale; Mid-Day*, exh, 1810; $35\frac{1}{2} \times 48$; Private Collection, England
118. (Cat. 109) *The Fall of an Avalanche in the Grisons*, exh. 1810; $35\frac{1}{2} \times 47\frac{1}{4}$; Tate Gallery
119. (Cat. 115) *Apollo and Python*, exh. 1811; $57\frac{1}{4} \times 93\frac{1}{2}$; Tate Gallery
120. (Cat. 113) *Petworth, Sussex, the Seat of the Earl of Egremont: Dewy Morning*, exh. 1810; $36 \times 47\frac{1}{2}$; Petworth House
121. (Cat. 116) *Somer-Hill, the Seat of W. F. Woodgate, Esq.*, exh. 1811; $36 \times 48\frac{1}{2}$; National Gallery of Scotland (Photo: Tom Scott)
122. (Cat. 114) *Mercury and Herse*, exh. 1811; 75×63; Private Collection, England
123. (Cat. 130) *Crossing the Brook*, exh. 1815; 76×65; Tate Gallery
124. (Cat. 117) *Whalley Bridge and Abbey, Lancashire: Dyers washing and drying Cloth*, exh. 1811; $24\frac{1}{8} \times 36\frac{3}{8}$; the Loyd Collection
125. (Cat. 121) *Saltash with the Water Ferry*, exh. 1812; $35\frac{3}{8} \times 47\frac{3}{4}$; The Metropolitan Museum of Art, New York. Gift of Henry G. Marquand, 1889
126. (Cat. 119) *Hulks on the Tamar*, exh. 1812?; $35\frac{1}{2} \times 47\frac{1}{2}$; Petworth House
127. (Cat. 120) *Teignmouth*, exh. 1812; $35\frac{1}{2} \times 47\frac{1}{2}$; Petworth House
128. (Cat. 122) *Ivy Bridge Mill, Devonshire*, exh. 1812; 35×47; Private Collection, England
129. (Cat. 123) St Mawes at the Pilchard Season, exh. 1812; $35\frac{7}{8} \times 47\frac{1}{2}$; Tate Gallery
130. (Cat. 125) *Oxford from the Abingdon Road*, exh. 1812; $26 \times 38\frac{1}{2}$; Private Collection, England
131. (Cat. 126) *Snow Storm: Hannibal and his Army crossing the Alps*, exh. 1812; $57\frac{1}{2} \times 93\frac{1}{2}$; Tate Gallery
132. (Cat. 127) *Frosty Morning*, exh. 1813; $44\frac{3}{4} \times 68\frac{3}{4}$;

Tate Gallery

133. (Cat. 131) *Dido building Carthage*, exh. 1815; $61\frac{1}{4} \times 91\frac{1}{4}$; reproduced by courtesy of the Trustees, The National Gallery, London
134. (Cat. 128) *Apullia in Search of Appulus*, exh. 1814; $57\frac{1}{2} \times 93\frac{7}{8}$; Tate Gallery
135. (Cat. 129) *Dido and Æneas*, exh. 1814; $57\frac{1}{2} \times 93\frac{3}{8}$; Tate Gallery
136. (Cat. 132) *The Eruption of the Souffrier Mountains*, exh. 1815; $31\frac{3}{4} \times 41\frac{1}{4}$; University of Liverpool
137. (Cat. 135) *The Decline of the Carthaginian Empire*, exh. 1817; 67×94; Tate Gallery
138. (Cat. 133) *The Temple of Jupiter Panellenius restored*, exh. 1816; 46×70; Private Collection, New York
139. (Cat. 134) *View of the Temple of Jupiter Panellenius, with the Greek National Dance of the Romaika*, exh. 1816; $46\frac{1}{4} \times 70$; the Duke of Northumberland, K.G.
140. (Cat. 137). *Dort, or Dordrecht: the Dort Packet-Boat from Rotterdam becalmed*, exh. 1818; 62×92; Yale Center for British Art, Paul Mellon Collection
141. (Cat. 138) *The Field of Waterloo*, exh. 1818; 58×94; Tate Gallery
142. (Cat. 136) *Raby Castle, the Seat of the Earl of Darlington*, exh. 1818; $46\frac{7}{8} \times 71\frac{1}{8}$; Walters Art Gallery, Baltimore
143. (Cat. 139) *Entrance of the Meuse: Orange-Merchant on the Bar, going to Pieces*, exh. 1819; 69×97; Tate Gallery
144. (Cat. 227) *Richmond Hill with Girls carrying Corn*, *c.* 1819; $58 \times 93\frac{3}{4}$; Tate Gallery
145. (Cat. 140) *England: Richmond Hill, on the Prince Regent's Birthday*, exh. 1819; $70\frac{7}{8} \times 131\frac{3}{4}$; Tate Gallery
146. (Cat. 141) *Conway Castle*, *c.* 1803; $40\frac{3}{4} \times 55$; Trustees of the Grosvenor Estate
147. (Cat. 142) *Fishing Boats entering Calais Harbour*, *c.* 1803; $29 \times 38\frac{3}{4}$; Copyright the Frick Collection, New York
148. (Cat. 143) *Seascape with a Squall coming up*, *c.* 1803–4; 18×24; from the collection of Malden Public Library, Malden, Massachusetts
149. (Cat. 144) *A Coast Scene with Fishermen hauling a Boat ashore (the 'Iveagh Seapiece')*, *c.* 1803–4; 36×48; The Greater London Council as Trustees of the Iveagh Bequest, Kenwood
150. (Cat. 145) *Fishmarket on the Beach*, *c.* 1802–4; $17\frac{1}{2} \times 23\frac{1}{4}$; R. F. Robertson-Glasgow, Esq.
151. (Cat. 145a) *Grenoble seen from the River Drac*, *c.* 1802–3; $14\frac{1}{4} \times 25\frac{1}{4}$; Tate Gallery
152. (Cat. 145b) *Mountain Scene with Castle, probably Martigny*, *c.* 1802–3; $17\frac{1}{4} \times 21\frac{1}{4}$; Tate Gallery
153. (Cat. 148) *Bonneville Savoy*, *c.* 1803–5; $13\frac{1}{4} \times 19\frac{1}{4}$; Present whereabouts unknown
154. (Cat. 147) *The Devil's Bridge, St Gothard*, *c.* 1803–4; $31\frac{3}{4} \times 24\frac{3}{4}$; Private Collection
155. (Cat. 146) *The Pass of St Gothard*, *c.* 1803–4; $31\frac{3}{4} \times 25\frac{1}{4}$; City Museums and Art Gallery, Birmingham
156. (Cat. 149) *Windsor Castle from the Thames*, *c.* 1805; $35\frac{3}{4} \times 48$; Petworth House
157. (Cat. 151) *Venus and the Dead Adonis*, *c.* 1805?; $12\frac{1}{2} \times 17\frac{3}{4}$; Tate Gallery
158. (Cat. 152) *The Procuress?*, *c.* 1805?; $47\frac{7}{8} \times 36$; Tate Gallery
159. (Cat. 153) *The Finding of Moses*, *c.* 1805?; $59\frac{1}{4} \times 44$; Tate Gallery
160. (Cat. 160) *Sketch for 'Harvest Dinner, Kingston Bank'*, *c.* 1806–7; 24×36; Tate Gallery
161. (Cat. 161) *Goring Mill and Church*, *c.* 1806–7; $33\frac{3}{4} \times 45\frac{3}{4}$; Tate Gallery
162. (Cat. 162) *Caversham Bridge*, *c.* 1806–7; $33\frac{5}{8} \times 45\frac{5}{8}$; Tate Gallery
163. (Cat. 163) *A Thames Backwater with Windsor Castle in the Distance*, *c.* 1806–7; $34\frac{1}{8} \times 47\frac{5}{8}$; Tate Gallery
164. (Cat. 164) *Hampton Court from the Thames*, *c.* 1806–7; $33\frac{3}{4} \times 47\frac{1}{4}$; Tate Gallery
165. (Cat. 165) *The Thames glimpsed between Trees, possibly at Kew Bridge*, *c.* 1806–7; $35\frac{7}{8} \times 47\frac{7}{8}$; Tate Gallery
166. (Cat. 166) *House beside the River*, *c.* 1806–7; $35\frac{5}{8} \times 45\frac{7}{8}$; Tate Gallery
167. (Cat. 167) *Weir and Cattle*, *c.* 1806–7; $34\frac{3}{4} \times 47\frac{1}{4}$; Tate Gallery
168. (Cat. 168) *Barge on the River, Sunset*, *c.* 1806–7; $33\frac{1}{2} \times 45\frac{3}{4}$; Tate Gallery
169. (Cat. 169) *Trees beside the River, with Bridge in the Middle Distance*, *c.* 1806–7; $34\frac{5}{8} \times 47\frac{1}{2}$; Tate Gallery
170. (Cat. 170) *Men with Horses crossing a River*, *c.* 1806–7; $34\frac{5}{8} \times 46\frac{5}{8}$; Tate Gallery
171. (Cat. 171) *River Scene with Weir in the Middle Distance*, *c.* 1806–7; $33\frac{5}{8} \times 45\frac{1}{2}$; Tate Gallery
172. (Cat. 172) *Willows beside a Stream*, *c.* 1806–7; $33\frac{7}{8} \times 45\frac{3}{4}$; Tate Gallery
173. (Cat. 173) *Washing Sheep*, *c.* 1806–7; $33\frac{1}{4} \times 45\frac{7}{8}$; Tate Gallery
174. (Cat. 174) *Margate, Setting Sun*, *c.* 1806–7; $33\frac{3}{4} \times 45\frac{3}{4}$; Tate Gallery
175. (Cat. 175) *Shipping at the Mouth of the Thames*, *c.* 1806–7; $33\frac{3}{4} \times 46$; Tate Gallery
176. (Cat. 176) *Coast Scene with Fishermen and Boats*, *c.* 1806–7; $33\frac{3}{4} \times 45\frac{3}{4}$; Tate Gallery
177. (Cat. 177) *Windsor Castle from Salt Hill*, *c.* 1807; $10\frac{7}{8} \times 29$; Tate Gallery
178. (Cat. 178) *Windsor from Lower Hope*, *c.* 1807; $12\frac{5}{8} \times 29$; Tate Gallery
179. (Cat. 179) *Windsor Castle from the Meadows*, *c.* 1807; $8\frac{3}{4} \times 21\frac{7}{8}$; Tate Gallery
180. (Cat. 180) *Windsor Castle from the River*, *c.* 1807; $7\frac{7}{8} \times 14\frac{7}{16}$; Tate Gallery
181. (Cat. 181) *Eton from the River*, *c.* 1807; $14\frac{1}{4} \times 26\frac{1}{8}$; Tate Gallery
182. (Cat. 182) *The Ford*, *c.* 1807; $14\frac{5}{8} \times 28\frac{15}{16}$; Tate Gallery
183. (Cat. 183) *The Thames near Windsor*, *c.* 1807;

$7\frac{3}{8} \times 10\frac{5}{16}$; Tate Gallery

184. (Cat. 184) *The Thames near Walton Bridges*, *c.* 1807; $14\frac{5}{8} \times 29$; Tate Gallery
185. (Cat. 185) *Walton Reach*, *c.* 1807; $14\frac{1}{2} \times 29$; Tate Gallery
186. (Cat. 186) *Tree Tops and Sky, Guildford Castle (?), Evening*, *c.* 1807; $10\frac{7}{8} \times 29$; Tate Gallery
187. (Cat. 187) *St Catherine's Hill, Guildford*, *c.* 1807; $14\frac{3}{8} \times 29$; Tate Gallery
188. (Cat. 188) *Guildford from the Banks of the Wey*, *c.* 1807; $10 \times 7\frac{3}{4}$; Tate Gallery
189. (Cat. 189) *A Narrow Valley*, *c.* 1807; $8\frac{1}{8} \times 6\frac{1}{2}$; Tate Gallery
190. (Cat. 190) *Godalming from the South*, *c.* 1807; $8 \times 13\frac{3}{4}$; Tate Gallery
191. (Cat. 191) *Newark Abbey*, *c.* 1807; $11\frac{5}{8} \times 13\frac{7}{8}$; Tate Gallery
192. (Cat. 192) *Newark Abbey on the Wey*, *c.* 1807; $14\frac{1}{2} \times 28\frac{15}{16}$; Tate Gallery
193. (Cat. 193) *On the Thames (?)*, *c.* 1807; $11\frac{5}{8} \times 13\frac{3}{4}$; Tate Gallery
194. (Cat. 194) *Sunset on the River*, *c.* 1807; $6\frac{1}{16} \times 7\frac{5}{16}$; Tate Gallery
195. (Cat. 195) *Windsor Park: Cows in a Woody Landscape*, *c.* 1805–7; $18\frac{3}{4} \times 28\frac{1}{4}$; Tate Gallery
196. (Cat. 196) *Cows in a Landscape with a Footbridge*, *c.* 1805–7; $18\frac{7}{8} \times 28$; Tate Gallery
197. (Cat. 197) *Hurley House on the Thames*, *c.* 1807–9; $15\frac{1}{2} \times 27$; Mrs M. V. Gairdner and others
198. (Cat. 198) *On the River Brent*, *c.* 1807–9; $14\frac{3}{4} \times 27$; Private Collection
199. (Cat. 200) *Cattle in a Stream under a Bridge*, *c.* 1805–7; $12\frac{3}{8} \times 15\frac{1}{2}$; Tate Gallery
200. (Cat. 201) *Newark Abbey*, *c.* 1807–8; 11×18; the Loyd Collection
201. (Cat. 204) *The Thames at Weybridge*, *c.* 1807–10; 35×47; Petworth House
202. (Cat. 203) *Gipsy Camp*, *c.* 1807–9; 48×36; Tate Gallery
203. (Cat. 206) Letter from Turner showing sketch for *Gravesend*, lower left, 1810. Picture untraced.
204. (Cat. 205) After *The Leader Sea Piece*, *c.* 1807–9; plate from the *Liber Studiorum*, 1809
205. (Cat. 207) *An Artists' Colourman's Workshop*, *c.* 1807; $24\frac{1}{2} \times 36$; Tate Gallery
206. (Cat. 208) *Tabley House*, 1808; $9 \times 11\frac{3}{4}$; British Museum
207. (Cat. 208a) *The Straw Yard*, *c.* 1808; $10\frac{3}{4} \times 16\frac{1}{4}$; Private Collection, Channel Islands
208. (Cat. 209) *Harvest Home*, *c.* 1809; $35\frac{5}{8} \times 47\frac{1}{2}$; Tate Gallery
209. (Cat. 209a) *Cassiobury Park: Reaping*, *c.* 1809; $35\frac{7}{16} \times 48$; Tate Gallery
210. (Cat. 211a) *English Landscape*, *c.* 1810; $7\frac{9}{16} \times 10\frac{1}{2}$; British Museum
211. (Cat. 212) *Mountain Stream, perhaps Bolton Glen*, *c.* 1810–15; $17\frac{5}{8} \times 23\frac{1}{4}$; Tate Gallery
212. (Cat. 211) *Rosehill Park, Sussex*, *c.* 1810; 35×47; Lt.-Col. Sir George Meyrick, Bt
213. (Cat. 210) *The Wreck of a Transport Ship*, *c.* 1810; 68×95; Fundaçao Calouste Gulbenkian, Lisbon
214. (Cat. 213) *Milton Combe (?)*, 1813; $6 \times 9\frac{1}{4}$; British Museum
215. (Cat. 214 recto) *Plympton*, 1813, $5\frac{1}{2} \times 9\frac{1}{4}$; British Museum
216. (Cat. 215) *Hamoaze from St John, Cornwall*, 1813; $6\frac{1}{4} \times 9\frac{1}{4}$; British Museum
217. (Cat. 216) *A Quarry, perhaps at Saltram*, 1813; $5\frac{1}{4} \times 9\frac{1}{4}$; British Museum
218. (Cat. 217) *The Plym Estuary from Boringdon Park*, 1813; $9\frac{1}{4} \times 11\frac{3}{4}$; British Museum
219. (Cat. 218) *A Bridge with a Cottage and Trees beyond*, 1813; $5\frac{7}{8} \times 9\frac{1}{4}$; British Museum
220. (Cat. 219) *Distant View of Plymouth from the North*, 1813; $5\frac{3}{4} \times 9\frac{1}{4}$; British Museum
221. (Cat. 220) *Plymouth from the North*, 1813; $4 \times 9\frac{1}{4}$; British Museum
222. (Cat. 221) *Shaugh Bridge, near Plymouth*, 1813; $6\frac{1}{4} \times 10\frac{1}{2}$; British Museum
223. (Cat. 222) *On the Plym Estuary near Crabtree*, 1813; $6 \times 9\frac{1}{4}$; British Museum
224. (Cat. 223) *Devonshire Bridge with Cottage*, 1813; $5\frac{15}{16} \times 9\frac{1}{4}$; British Museum
225. (Cat. 224) *The Plym Estuary looking North*, 1813, $5\frac{3}{4} \times 9\frac{1}{4}$; British Museum
226. (Cat. 225) *A Valley in Devonshire*, 1813; $7\frac{5}{8} \times 10\frac{3}{8}$; Leeds City Art Galleries
227. (Cat. 225a) *View over Plymouth Harbour*, 1813; $6 \times 9\frac{1}{4}$; Private Collection, U.S.A
228. (Cat. 214 verso) *Landscape Study*, 1813; $6\frac{1}{2} \times 5\frac{1}{2}$; British Museum
229. (Cat. 226a) *An Evening Scene*, *c.* 1815?; $3 \times 5\frac{1}{8}$; British Museum
230. (Cat. 225b) *A Devonshire Valley*, 1813; $6\frac{1}{4} \times 9\frac{3}{4}$; Private Collection, U.S.A.
231. (Cat. 228) *Rome, from the Vatican*, exh. 1820; $69\frac{3}{4} \times 132$; Tate Gallery
232. (Cat. 229) *What You Will!*, exh. 1822; $19 \times 20\frac{1}{2}$; Sir Michael Sobell
233. (Cat. 230) *The Bay of Baiae, with Apollo and the Sybil*, exh. 1823; $57\frac{1}{4} \times 94$; Tate Gallery
234. (Cat. 231) *Harbour of Dieppe (Changement de Domicile)*, exh. 1825; $68\frac{3}{8} \times 88\frac{3}{4}$; Copyright the Frick Collection, New York
235. (Cat. 232) *Cologne, the Arrival of a Packet Boat, Evening*, exh. 1826; $66\frac{3}{8} \times 88\frac{1}{4}$; Copyright the Frick Collection, New York
236. (Cat. 235) *The Seat of William Moffatt, Esq., at Mortlake. Early (Summer's) Morning*, exh. 1826; $36\frac{5}{8} \times 48\frac{1}{2}$; Copyright the Frick Collection, New York
237. (Cat. 239) *Mortlake Terrace, the Seat of William Moffatt, Esq. Summer's Evening*, exh. 1827; $36\frac{1}{4} \times 48\frac{1}{8}$; National Gallery of Art, Washington, D.C., Andrew W. Mellon Collection
238. (Cat. 233) *Forum Romanum*, exh. 1826; $57\frac{3}{8} \times 93$; Tate Gallery
239. (Cat. 236) *'Now for the Painter'. Passengers going on Board*, exh. 1827; 67×88; City of Manchester Art Galleries

240. (Cat. 234) *View from the Terrace of a Villa at Niton*, exh. 1826; $17\frac{3}{4} \times 23\frac{1}{2}$; Mr William A. Coolidge
241. (Cat. 269) *Near Northcourt in the Isle of Wight*, *c.* 1827; $17\frac{1}{4} \times 24\frac{1}{8}$; Musée de Québec
242. (Cat. 237) *Port Ruysdael*, exh. 1827; $36\frac{1}{4} \times 48\frac{1}{4}$; Yale Center for British Art, Paul Mellon Collection
243. (Cat. 241) *Dido directing the Equipment of the Fleet*, exh. 1828; 59×89; Tate Gallery (from pre-1917 photograph)
244. (Cat. 238) *Rembrandt's Daughter*, exh. 1827; 48×34; Courtesy of the Fogg Art Museum, Harvard University, Cambridge, Mass. Gift of Edward W. Forbes
245. (Cat. 244) *Boccaccio relating the Tale of the Bird-cage*, exh. 1828; $48 \times 35\frac{5}{8}$; Tate Gallery
246. (Cat. 242) *East Cowes Castle, the Seat of J. Nash, Esq.; the Regatta beating to Windward*, exh. 1828; $35\frac{1}{2} \times 47\frac{1}{2}$; Indianapolis Museum of Art. Gift of Mr and Mrs Nicholas Noyes (Photo: Robert Wallace)
247. (Cat. 243) *East Cowes Castle, the Seat of J. Nash, Esq.; the Regatta starting for their Moorings*, exh. 1828; $36 \times 48\frac{1}{2}$; by courtesy of the Victoria and Albert Museum
248. (Cat. 245) *The Rialto, Venice*, *c.* 1820; $69\frac{7}{8} \times 132$; Tate Gallery
249. (Cat. 246) *An Avenue of Trees*, *c.* 1822?; $19\frac{1}{2} \times 21\frac{1}{8}$; Tate Gallery
250. (Cat. 247) *George IV at St Giles's, Edinburgh*, *c.* 1822; $29\frac{11}{16} \times 36\frac{1}{8}$; Tate Gallery
251. (Cat. 248) *George IV at the Provost's Banquet, Edinburgh*, *c.* 1822; $27 \times 36\frac{1}{8}$; Tate Gallery
252. (Cat. 248a) *Sir Walter Scott going out to meet George IV*, *c.* 1822; $26\frac{3}{4} \times 36\frac{1}{8}$; Tate Gallery
253. (Cat. 248b) *George IV's Departure from the 'Royal George'*, *c.* 1822; $29\frac{5}{8} \times 36\frac{3}{16}$; Tate Gallery
254. (Cat. 249) *Scene in a Church or Vaulted Hall*, *c.* 1820–30; $29\frac{1}{2} \times 39$; Tate Gallery
255. (Cat. 252) *The Battle of Trafalgar*, 1822–4; 102×144; National Maritime Museum, Greenwich
256. (Cat. 250) *First Sketch for 'The Battle of Trafalgar'*, *c.* 1822–3; $35\frac{1}{2} \times 47\frac{3}{4}$; Tate Gallery
257. (Cat. 251) *Second Sketch for 'The Battle of Trafalgar'*, *c.* 1822–3; $35\frac{1}{2} \times 47\frac{3}{4}$; Tate Gallery
258. (Cat. 253) *Tynemouth Priory*, *c.* 1820–25?; $12\frac{1}{2} \times 24$; Tate Gallery
259. (Cat. 254) *View on the Avon*, *c.* 1825; $15 \times 20\frac{7}{8}$; Private Collection, England
260. (Cat. 259a) *Storm off the Farne Islands*, *c.* 1825?; $5\frac{3}{4} \times 8$; present whereabouts unknown (from old photograph)
261. (Cat. 256) *Valley with a Distant Bridge and Tower*, *c.* 1825; $35\frac{7}{8} \times 48\frac{1}{8}$; Tate Gallery
262. (Cat. 257) *Landscape Composition*, *c.* 1820–30; $21\frac{5}{8} \times 29\frac{1}{2}$; Tate Gallery
263. (Cat. 258) *The Cobbler's Home*, *c.* 1825; $23\frac{1}{2} \times 31\frac{1}{2}$; Tate Gallery
264. (Cat. 259) *Death on a Pale Horse (?)*, *c.* 1825–30; $23\frac{1}{2} \times 29\frac{3}{4}$; Tate Gallery
265. (Cat. 260) *Sketch for 'East Cowes Castle, the Regatta beating to Windward' no. 1*, 1827; $11\frac{3}{4} \times 19\frac{1}{4}$; Tate Gallery
266. (Cat. 261) *Sketch for 'East Cowes Castle, the Regatta beating to Windward' no. 2*, 1827; $17\frac{3}{4} \times 23\frac{7}{8}$; Tate Gallery
267. (Cat. 262) *Sketch for 'East Cowes Castle, the Regatta beating to Windward' no. 3*, 1827; $18\frac{1}{4} \times 28\frac{1}{2}$; Tate Gallery
268. (Cat. 263) *Sketch for 'East Cowes Castle, the Regatta starting for their Moorings' no. 1*, 1827; $18\frac{1}{8} \times 23\frac{7}{8}$; Tate Gallery
269. (Cat. 264) *Sketch for 'East Cowes Castle, the Regatta starting for their Moorings' no. 2*, 1827; $17\frac{1}{2} \times 29$; Tate Gallery
270. (Cat. 265) *Sketch for 'East Cowes Castle, the Regatta starting for their Moorings' no. 3*, 1827; $17\frac{3}{4} \times 24$; Tate Gallery
271. (Cat. 266) *Between Decks*, 1827; $12 \times 19\frac{1}{8}$; Tate Gallery
272. (Cat. 267) *Shipping off East Cowes Headland*, 1827; $18\frac{1}{8} \times 23\frac{3}{4}$; Tate Gallery
273. (Cat. 268) *Study of Sea and Sky, Isle of Wight*, 1827; $12 \times 19\frac{1}{8}$; Tate Gallery
274. (Cat. 272) *A Sandy Beach*, *c.* 1825–30; $25\frac{5}{8} \times 36$; Tate Gallery
275. (Cat. 273) *Rocky Coast*, *c.* 1825–30; $19\frac{3}{4} \times 25\frac{7}{8}$; Tate Gallery
276. (Cat. 274) *Seascape with a Yacht (?)*, *c.* 1825–30; $19\frac{3}{4} \times 26$; Tate Gallery
277. (Cat. 275) *Seascape with Sailing Boat and a Ship*, *c.* 1825–30; $18\frac{3}{8} \times 24$; Tate Gallery
278. (Cat. 276) *Lake or River with Trees on the Right*, *c.* 1825–30; $16\frac{1}{4} \times 23\frac{1}{2}$; Tate Gallery
279. (Cat. 279) *Steamer and Lightship*, *c.* 1825–30; $36 \times 47\frac{7}{8}$; Tate Gallery
280. (Cat. 280) *Two Compositions: A Claudian Seaport and an Open Landscape*, *c.* 1825–30; $13\frac{1}{4} \times 23\frac{3}{4}$; Tate Gallery
281. (Cat. 328) *Italian Landscape with a Tower*, *c.* 1825–30; 23×30; Tate Gallery
282. (Cat. 271) *Three Seascapes*, *c.* 1827; $35\frac{3}{4} \times 23\frac{3}{4}$; Tate Gallery
283. (Cat. 441) *Studies for 'Dawn of Christianity'*, *c.* 1841; $52\frac{5}{8} \times 25\frac{5}{8}$; Tate Gallery
284. (Cat. 282) *Evening Landscape, probably Chichester Canal*, *c.* 1825–8; $25\frac{1}{2} \times 49\frac{1}{2}$; Tate Gallery
285. (Cat. 283) *Petworth Park: Tillington Church in the Distance*, *c.* 1828; $25\frac{3}{8} \times 57\frac{3}{8}$; Tate Gallery
286. (Cat. 284) *The Lake, Petworth, Sunset*, *c.* 1828; $25\frac{1}{2} \times 55\frac{1}{2}$; Tate Gallery
287. (Cat. 285) *Chichester Canal*, *c.* 1828; $25\frac{3}{4} \times 53$; Tate Gallery
288. (Cat. 286) *The Chain Pier, Brighton*, *c.* 1828; $28 \times 53\frac{3}{4}$; Tate Gallery
289. (Cat. 287) *A Ship aground*, *c.* 1828; $27\frac{1}{2} \times 53\frac{1}{2}$; Tate Gallery
290. (Cat. 288) *The Lake, Petworth: Sunset, Fighting*

Bucks, *c.* 1829; $24\frac{1}{2} \times 57\frac{1}{2}$; Petworth House

291. (Cat. 289) *The Lake, Petworth: Sunset, a Stag drinking*, *c.* 1829; 25×52; Petworth House
292. (Cat. 290) *Chichester Canal*, *c.* 1829; 25×52; Petworth House
293. (Cat. 291) *Brighton from the Sea*, *c.* 1829; 25×52; Petworth House
294. (Cat. 292) *View of Orvieto*, 1828 (reworked 1830); $36 \times 48\frac{1}{2}$; Tate Gallery
295. (Cat. 293) *Vision of Medea*, 1828; $68\frac{3}{8} \times 98$; Tate Gallery
296. (Cat. 294) *Regulus*, 1828 (reworked 1837); $35\frac{1}{4} \times 48\frac{3}{4}$; Tate Gallery
297. (Cat. 295) *Palestrina—Composition*, 1828; $55\frac{1}{4} \times 98$; Tate Gallery
298. (Cat. 296) *Reclining Venus*, 1828; 69×98; Tate Gallery
299. (Cat. 297) *Two Recumbent Nude Figures*, 1828; $68\frac{3}{4} \times 98\frac{1}{8}$; Tate Gallery
300. (Cat. 298) *Outline of the Venus Pudica*, 1828; $53\frac{3}{8} \times 38\frac{5}{8}$; Tate Gallery
301. (Cat. 281) *Landscape with a Castle on a Promontory*, *c.* 1820–30?; $19\frac{1}{4} \times 15\frac{7}{8}$; Tate Gallery
302. (Cat. 299) *Southern Landscape*, 1828; $69\frac{1}{2} \times 99\frac{1}{8}$; Tate Gallery
303. (Cat. 300) *Southern Landscape with an Aqueduct and Waterfall*, 1828; $59\frac{1}{8} \times 98\frac{1}{8}$; Tate Gallery
304. (Cat. 301) *Italian Landscape, probably Civita di Bagnoregio*, 1828; $59 \times 98\frac{1}{4}$; Tate Gallery
305. (Cat. 302) *Sketch for 'Ulysses deriding Polyphemus'*, 1828; $23\frac{5}{8} \times 35\frac{1}{8}$; Tate Gallery
306. (Cat. 303) *Italian Bay*, 1828; $23\frac{3}{4} \times 40\frac{1}{4}$; Tate Gallery
307. (Cat. 304) *Lake Nemi*, 1828; $23\frac{3}{4} \times 39\frac{1}{4}$; Tate Gallery
308. (Cat. 305) *Ariccia (?): Sunset*, 1828; $23\frac{7}{8} \times 31\frac{1}{4}$; Tate Gallery
309. (Cat. 306) *Overlooking the Coast, with Classical Buildings*, 1828; $23\frac{3}{4} \times 33\frac{1}{4}$; Tate Gallery
310. (Cat. 307) *Italian Landscape with Tower, Trees and Figures*, 1828; $23\frac{5}{8} \times 34\frac{7}{8}$; Tate Gallery
311. (Cat. 308) *Classical Harbour Scene*, 1828; $23\frac{3}{4} \times 40\frac{1}{8}$; Tate Gallery
312. (Cat. 309) *Rocky Bay*, 1828; $23\frac{3}{4} \times 36\frac{1}{4}$; Tate Gallery
313. (Cat. 310) *Archway with Trees by the Sea*, 1828; $23\frac{5}{8} \times 34\frac{1}{4}$; Tate Gallery
314. (Cat. 311) *Tivoli, the Cascatelle*, 1828; $23\frac{7}{8} \times 30\frac{5}{8}$; Tate Gallery
315. (Cat. 312) *Italian Landscape with Bridge and Tower*, 1828; $23\frac{3}{4} \times 38\frac{5}{8}$; Tate Gallery
316. (Cat. 313) *Claudian Harbour Scene*, 1828; $23\frac{5}{8} \times 36\frac{7}{8}$; Tate Gallery
317. (Cat. 314) *Stack and Fire (?)*, 1828; $23\frac{5}{8} \times 33\frac{3}{8}$; Tate Gallery
318. (Cat. 315) *A Park*, 1828; $23\frac{3}{4} \times 38\frac{7}{8}$; Tate Gallery
319. (Cat. 316) *Scene on the Banks of a River*, 1828; $23\frac{3}{4} \times 35\frac{1}{8}$; Tate Gallery
320. (Cat. 317) *Fishing Boat in a Mist*, 1828; $23\frac{3}{4} \times 35\frac{3}{4}$; Tate Gallery
321. (Cat. 318) *Hilltown on the Edge of the Campagna*, 1828?; $16\frac{1}{8} \times 23\frac{3}{8}$; Tate Gallery
322. (Cat. 319) *Seacoast with Ruin, probably the Bay of Baiae*, 1828?; $16\frac{1}{4} \times 23\frac{11}{16}$; Tate Gallery
323. (Cat. 320) *Coast Scene near Naples*, 1828?; $16\frac{1}{8} \times 23\frac{1}{2}$; Tate Gallery
324. (Cat. 321) *Landscape with Trees and a Castle*, 1828?; $16\frac{5}{16} \times 23\frac{5}{8}$; Tate Gallery
325. (Cat. 322) *Mountainous Landscape*, 1828?; $16\frac{1}{4} \times 23\frac{1}{2}$; Tate Gallery
326. (Cat. 323) *Hilly Landscape with Tower* (?) 1828?; $16\frac{9}{16} \times 20\frac{5}{8}$; Tate Gallery
327. (Cat. 324) *Landscape with a Tree on the Right*, 1828?; $11 \times 16\frac{3}{8}$; Tate Gallery
328. (Cat. 325) *Seascape with Burning Hulk*, 1828?; $9\frac{1}{2} \times 16\frac{3}{8}$; Tate Gallery
329. (Cat. 326) *A Seashore*, 1828?; $16\frac{3}{8} \times 20\frac{1}{2}$; Tate Gallery
330. (Cat. 327) *Seascape*, 1828?; $16\frac{1}{2} \times 20\frac{1}{2}$; Tate Gallery
331. (Cat. 330) *Ulysses deriding Polyphemus*, exh. 1829; $52\frac{1}{4} \times 80$; reproduced by courtesy of the Trustees, The National Gallery, London
332. (Cat. 328a) *A View on the Rhone (?)*, *c.* 1828–9; $27\frac{15}{16} \times 20\frac{7}{8}$; Worcester Art Museum, Worcester, Mass.
333. (Cat. 333) *Jessica*, exh. 1830; 48×36; Petworth House
334. (Cat. 331) *The Loretto Necklace*, exh. 1829; $51\frac{1}{2} \times 68\frac{7}{8}$; Tate Gallery
335. (Cat. 332) *Pilate Washing his Hands*, exh. 1830; 36×48; Tate Gallery
336. (Cat. 334). *Calais Sands, Low Water, Poissards collecting Bait*, exh. 1830; $28\frac{1}{2} \times 42$; Bury Art Gallery
337. (Cat. 335) *Fish-Market on the Sands—the Sun Rising through a Vapour*, exh. 1830; 34×44; destroyed
338. (Cat. 336) *Life-Boat and Manby Apparatus going off to a Stranded Vessel making Signal (Blue Lights) of Distress*, exh. 1831; 36×48; by courtesy of the Victoria and Albert Museum
339. (Cat. 337) *Caligula's Palace and Bridge*, exh. 1831; 54×97; Tate Gallery
340. (Cat. 338) *Lucy, Countess of Carlisle, and Dorothy Percy's Visit to their Father Lord Percy, when under Attainder*, exh. 1831; $15\frac{3}{4} \times 27\frac{1}{4}$; Tate Gallery
341. (Cat. 340) *Watteau Study by Fresnoy's Rules*, exh. 1831; $15\frac{3}{4} \times 27\frac{1}{4}$; Tate Gallery
342. (Cat. 339) *Admiral Van Tromp's Barge at the Entrance of the Texel, 1645*, exh. 1831; $35\frac{1}{2} \times 48$; Trustees of Sir John Soane's Museum, London
343. (Cat. 341) *Fort Vimieux*, exh. 1831; 28×42; Private Collection, England
344. (Cat. 342) *Childe Harold's Pilgrimage—Italy*, exh. 1832; $56 \times 97\frac{3}{4}$; Tate Gallery
345. (Cat. 343) *The Prince of Orange, William III, embarked from Holland, and landed at Torbay, November 4th, 1688*, exh. 1832; $35\frac{1}{2} \times 47\frac{1}{4}$; Tate

Gallery
346. (Cat. 344) *Van Tromp's Shallop, at the Entrance of the Scheldt*, exh. 1832; 35 × 47; Wadsworth Atheneum, Hartford, Connecticut
347. (Cat. 345) *Helvoetsluys;—the City of Utrecht, 64, going to Sea*, exh. 1832; 36 × 48; Private Collection, London
348. (Cat. 346) *Shadrach, Meshech and Abednego in the Burning Fiery Furnace*, exh. 1832; $36\frac{1}{16} \times 27\frac{7}{8}$; Tate Gallery
349. (Cat. 436) *Christ driving the Traders from the Temple*, c. 1832; $36\frac{1}{4} \times 27\frac{3}{4}$; Tate Gallery
350. (Cat. 347) *Staffa, Fingal's Cave*, exh. 1832; 36 × 48; Yale Center for British Art, Paul Mellon Collection
351. (Cat. 348) *Rotterdam Ferry Boat*, exh. 1833; $36\frac{1}{2} \times 48\frac{1}{2}$; National Gallery of Art, Washington, D.C., Ailsa Mellon Bruce Collection
352. (Cat. 526) *A Mountain Lake at Sunset*, c. 1830–35; $9\frac{1}{4} \times 6\frac{1}{8}$; Mr William Wood Prince, Chicago
353. (Cat. 352) After *Ducal Palace, Venice*, exh. 1833; engraving by W. Miller, 1854
354. (Cat. 350) *Van Goyen, looking out for a Subject*, exh. 1833; $36\frac{1}{2} \times 48\frac{3}{8}$; Copyright the Frick Collection, New York
355. (Cat. 351) *Van Tromp returning after the Battle off the Dogger Bank*, exh. 1833; $35\frac{5}{8} \times 47\frac{1}{2}$; Tate Gallery
356. (Cat. 349) *Bridge of Sighs, Ducal Palace and Custom-House, Venice: Canaletti painting*, exh. 1833; $20\frac{3}{16} \times 32\frac{7}{16}$; Tate Gallery
357. (Cat. 353) *Mouth of the Seine, Quille-Boeuf*, exh. 1833; $36 \times 48\frac{1}{2}$; Fundaçao Calouste Gulbenkian, Lisbon
358. (Cat. 354) *The Fountain of Indolence*, exh. 1834; $42 \times 65\frac{1}{2}$; the Beaverbrook Foundation, photo, courtesy of the Beaverbrook Art Gallery, Frederiction, New Brunswick, Canada
359. (Cat. 355) *The Golden Bough*, exh. 1834; $41 \times 64\frac{1}{2}$; Tate Gallery
360. (Cat. 357) *Wreckers,—Coast of Northumberland*, exh. 1834; 36 × 48; Yale Center for British Art, Paul Mellon Collection
361. (Cat. 358) *St Michael's Mount, Cornwall*, exh. 1834; $24 \times 30\frac{1}{2}$; by courtesy of the Victoria and Albert Museum
362. (Cat. 356) *Venice*, exh. 1834; $35\frac{1}{2} \times 48$; National Gallery of Art, Washington, D.C., Widener Collection
363. (Cat. 360) *Keelmen heaving in Coals by Night*, exh. 1835; $35\frac{1}{2} \times 48$; National Gallery of Art, Washington, D.C., Widener Collection
364. (Cat. 359) *The Burning of the House of Lords and Commons, 16th October, 1834*, exh. 1835; $36\frac{1}{4} \times 48\frac{1}{2}$; Philadelphia Museum of Art
365. (Cat. 364) *The Burning of the Houses of Lords and Commons, October 16, 1834*, exh. 1835; $36\frac{1}{2} \times 48\frac{1}{2}$; the Cleveland Museum of Art. Bequest of John L. Severance
366. (Cat. 361) *The Bright Stone of Honour (Ehrenbreitstein)*, exh. 1835; $36\frac{1}{2} \times 48\frac{1}{2}$; Private Collection, London
367. (Cat. 362) *Venice, from the Porch of Madonna della Salute*, exh. 1835; 36 × 48; The Metropolitan Museum of Art, New York. Bequest of Cornelius Vanderbilt II, 1899
368. (Cat. 363) *Line-Fishing, off Hastings*, exh. 1835; 23 × 30; by courtesy of the Victoria and Albert Museum
369. (Cat. 365) *Juliet and her Nurse*, exh. 1836; $36\frac{1}{2} \times 48\frac{1}{2}$; Sra. Amalia Lacroze de Fortabat, Argentina
370. (Cat. 366) *Rome, from Mount Aventine*, exh. 1836; 36 × 49; the Earl of Rosebery
371. (Cat. 369) *Story of Apollo and Daphne*, exh. 1837; $43\frac{1}{4} \times 78\frac{1}{4}$; Tate Gallery
372. (Cat. 367) *Mercury and Argus*, exh. 1836; 59 × 43; National Gallery of Canada, Ottawa
373. (Cat. 368) *The Grand Canal, Venice*, exh. 1837; $58\frac{1}{4} \times 43\frac{1}{2}$; Henry E. Huntington Library and Art Gallery, San Marino, California
374. (Cat. 370) *The Parting of Hero and Leander*, exh. 1837; $57\frac{1}{2} \times 93$; reproduced by courtesy of the Trustees, The National Gallery, London
375. (Cat. 371) *Snow-Storm, Avalanche and Inundation—a Scene in the Upper Part of Val d'Aouste, Piedmont*, exh. 1837; $36\frac{1}{4} \times 48$; courtesy of the Art Institute of Chicago
376. (Cat. 374) *Modern Italy—the Pifferari*, exh. 1838; $36\frac{1}{2} \times 48\frac{1}{2}$; Glasgow Art Gallery
377. (Cat. 375) *Ancient Italy—Ovid banished from Rome*, exh. 1838; $37\frac{1}{4} \times 49\frac{1}{4}$; Private Collection
378. (Cat. 373) *Phryne going to the Public Baths as Venus*, exh. 1838; 76 × 65; Tate Gallery
379. (Cat. 382) *Bacchus and Ariadne*, exh. 1840; 31 × 31; Tate Gallery
380. (Cat. 372) *Fishing Boats with Hucksters bargaining for Fish*, exh. 1838; $65\frac{5}{8} \times 88\frac{1}{4}$; courtesy of the Art Institue of Chicago
381. (Cat. 377) *The Fighting 'Temeraire', tugged to her Last Berth to be broken up, 1838*, exh. 1839; $35\frac{1}{4} \times 48$; reproduced by courtesy of the Trustees, The National Gallery, London
382. (Cat. 378) *Ancient Rome; Agrippina landing with the Ashes of Germanicus*, exh. 1839; 36 × 48; Tate Gallery
383. (Cat. 379) *Modern Rome—Campo Vaccino*, exh. 1839; $35\frac{1}{2} \times 48$; the Earl of Rosebery
384. (Cat. 380) *Pluto carrying off Proserpine*, exh. 1839; $36\frac{5}{8} \times 48\frac{5}{8}$; National Gallery of Art, Washington, D.C., Gift of Mrs Watson B. Dickerman
385. (Cat. 381) *Cicero at his Villa*, exh. 1839; $36\frac{1}{2} \times 48\frac{1}{2}$; Evelyn de Rothschild Esq., Ascott, Bucks.
386. (Cat. 383) *Venice, the Bridge of Sighs*, exh. 1840; 24 × 36; Tate Gallery
387. (Cat. 384) *Venice, from the Canale della Giudecca, Chiesa di S. Maria della Salute*, exh. 1840; 24 × 36; by courtesy of the Victoria and Albert Museum

388. (Cat. 385) *Slavers throwing overboard the Dead and Dying*, exh. 1840; $35\frac{3}{4} \times 48$; Museum of Fine Arts, Boston. Purchased, Henry Lillie Pierce Fund
389. (Cat. 386) *The New Moon; or 'I've lost my Boat, You shan't have your Hoop'*, exh. 1840; $25\frac{3}{4} \times 32$; Tate Gallery
390. (Cat. 388) *Neapolitan Fisher-Girls surprised bathing by Moonlight*, exh. 1840?; $25\frac{5}{8} \times 31\frac{5}{8}$; Henry E. Huntington Library and Art Gallery, San Marino, California
391. (Cat. 389) *Neapolitan Fisher-Girls surprised bathing by Moonlight*, exh. 1840?; 25×31; Private Collection, U.S.A.
392. (Cat. 387) *Rockets and Blue Lights (close at Hand) to warn Steam-Boats of Shoal-Water*, exh. 1840; $35\frac{1}{2} \times 47$; Sterling and Francine Clark Art Institute, Williamstown, Mass.
393. (Cat. 393) *Depositing of John Bellini's Three Pictures in la Chiesa Redentore, Venice*, exh. 1841; $29 \times 45\frac{1}{2}$; Private Collection
394. (Cat. 390) *Ducal Palace, Dogano, with Part of San Georgio, Venice*, exh. 1841; $25 \times 36\frac{5}{8}$; Allen Memorial Art Museum, Oberlin College
395. (Cat. 391) *Giudecca, la Donna della Salute and San Georgio*, exh. 1841; 24×36; Mr William Wood Prince and the Art Institute of Chicago
396. (Cat. 392) *Schloss Rosenau, Seat of H.R.H. Prince Albert of Coburg*, exh. 1841; $38\frac{1}{4} \times 49\frac{1}{8}$; Walker Art Gallery, Liverpool
397. (Cat. 442) *Rosenau*, *c.* 1841–4; 38×49; Yale Center for British Art, Paul Mellon Collection
398. (Cat. 394) *Dawn of Christianity (Flight into Egypt)*, exh. 1841; 31×31; Ulster Museum, Belfast
399. (Cat. 395) *Glaucus and Scylla*, exh. 1841; $31 \times 30\frac{1}{2}$; Kimbell Art Museum, Fort Worth, Texas
400. (Cat. 396) *The Dogano, San Giorgio, Citella, from the Steps of the Europa*, exh. 1842; $24\frac{1}{2} \times 36\frac{1}{2}$; Tate Gallery
401. (Cat. 397) *Campo Santo, Venice*, exh. 1842; $24\frac{1}{2} \times 36\frac{1}{2}$; Toledo Museum of Art, Toledo, Ohio. Gift of Edward Drummond Libbey
402. (Cat. 399) *Peace—Burial at Sea*, exh. 1842; $34\frac{1}{4} \times 34\frac{1}{8}$; Tate Gallery
403. (Cat. 400) *War. The Exile and the Rock Limpet*, exh. 1842; $31\frac{1}{4} \times 31\frac{1}{4}$; Tate Gallery
404. (Cat. 398) *Snow Storm—Steam-Boat off a Harbour's Mouth*, exh. 1842; 36×48; Tate Gallery
405. (Cat. 443) *The Evening of the Deluge*, *c.* 1843; $29\frac{7}{8} \times 29\frac{7}{8}$; National Gallery of Art, Washinghton, D.C., Timken Collection
406. (Cat. 404) *Shade and Darkness—the Evening of the Deluge*, exh. 1843; $31 \times 30\frac{3}{4}$; Tate Gallery
407. (Cat. 405) *Light and Colour (Goethe's Theory)—the Morning after the Deluge—Moses writing the Book of Genesis*, exh. 1843; 31×31; Tate Gallery
408. (Cat. 402) *The Sun of Venice going to Sea*, exh. 1843; $24\frac{1}{4} \times 36\frac{1}{4}$; Tate Gallery
409. (Cat. 403) *Dogana, and Madonna della Salute, Venice*, exh. 1843; $24\frac{3}{4} \times 36\frac{5}{8}$; National Gallery of Art, Washington, D.C., Given in memory of Governor Alvan T. Fuller by the Fuller Foundation
410. (Cat. 401) *The Opening of the Walhalla, 1842*, exh. 1843; $44\frac{5}{16} \times 79$; Tate Gallery
411. (Cat. 406) *St Benedetto, looking towards Fusina*, exh. 1843; $24\frac{1}{2} \times 36\frac{1}{2}$; Tate Gallery
412. (Cat. 407) *Ostend*, exh. 1844; $36\frac{1}{2} \times 48\frac{1}{2}$; Neue Pinakothek, Munich
413. (Cat. 408) *Fishing Boats bringing a Disabled Ship into Port Ruysdael*, exh. 1844; $36 \times 48\frac{1}{2}$; Tate Gallery
414. (Cat. 409) *Rain, Steam, and Speed—the Great Western Railway*, exh. 1844; $35\frac{3}{4} \times 48$; reproduced by courtesy of the Trustees, The National Gallery, London
415. (Cat. 410) *Van Tromp, going about to please his Masters*, exh. 1844; 36×48; Royal Holloway College, University of London
416. (Cat. 411) *Venice—Maria della Salute*, exh. 1844; $24\frac{1}{8} \times 36\frac{1}{4}$; Tate Gallery
417. (Cat. 412) *Approach to Venice*, exh. 1844; $24\frac{1}{2} \times 37$; National Gallery of Art, Washington, D.C., Andrew W. Mellon Collection
418. (Cat. 413) *Venice Quay, Ducal Palace*, exh. 1844; $24\frac{1}{2} \times 36\frac{1}{2}$; Tate Gallery
419. (Cat. 420) *Queen Mab's Cave*, exh. 1846; $36\frac{1}{4} \times 48\frac{1}{4}$; Tate Gallery
420. (Cat. 416) *Venice, Evening, going to the Ball*, exh. 1845; $24\frac{1}{4} \times 36\frac{3}{8}$; Tate Gallery
421. (Cat. 417) *Morning, returning from the Ball, St. Martino*, exh. 1845; $24\frac{1}{2} \times 36\frac{1}{2}$; Tate Gallery
422. (Cat. 418) *Venice—Noon*, exh. 1845; $24 \times 36\frac{1}{8}$; Tate Gallery
423. (Cat. 419) *Venice—Sunset, a Fisher*, exh. 1845; $24\frac{1}{8} \times 36\frac{1}{4}$; Tate Gallery
424. (Cat. 414) *Whalers*, exh. 1845; $35\frac{7}{8} \times 48$; Tate Gallery
425. (Cat. 415) *Whalers*, exh. 1845; $36\frac{1}{8} \times 48\frac{1}{4}$; The Metropolitan Museum of Art, New York, Wolfe Fund, 1896
426. (Cat. 423) *'Hurrah! for the Whaler Erebus! another Fish!'*, exh. 1846; $35\frac{1}{2} \times 47\frac{1}{2}$; Tate Gallery
427. (Cat. 426) *Whalers (boiling Blubber) entangled in Flaw Ice*, exh. 1846; $35\frac{3}{8} \times 47\frac{1}{4}$; Tate Gallery
428. (Cat. 421) *Going to the Ball (San Martino)*, exh. 1846; 24×36; Oakpict Inc.
429. (Cat. 422) *Returning from the Ball (St Martha)*, exh. 1846; 24×36; Oakpict Inc.
430. (Cat. 424) *Undine giving the Ring to Massaniello, Fisherman of Naples*, exh. 1846; $31\frac{1}{8} \times 31\frac{1}{8}$; Tate Gallery
431. (Cat. 425) *The Angel standing in the Sun*, exh. 1846; 31×31; Tate Gallery
432. (Cat. 427) *The Hero of a Hundred Fights*, *c.* 1800–10 (reworked and exh. 1847); $35\frac{3}{4} \times 47\frac{3}{4}$; Tate Gallery

433. (Cat. 428) *The Wreck Buoy*, *c.* 1807 (reworked and exh. 1849); $36\frac{1}{2} \times 48\frac{1}{2}$; Walker Art Gallery, Liverpool
434. (Cat. 429) *Mercury sent to admonish Æneas*, exh. 1850; $35\frac{1}{2} \times 47\frac{1}{2}$; Tate Gallery
435. (Cat. 430) *Æneas relating his Story to Dido*, exh. 1850; 36 × 48; destroyed?, formerly Tate Gallery (from 1906 reproduction)
436. (Cat. 431) *The Visit to the Tomb*, exh. 1850; 36 × 48; Tate Gallery
437. (Cat. 432) *The Departure of the Fleet*, exh. 1850; $35\frac{3}{8} \times 47\frac{3}{8}$; Tate Gallery
438. (Cat. 433) *Landscape: Christ and the Woman of Samaria*, *c.* 1830; $57\frac{1}{4} \times 93\frac{1}{2}$; Tate Gallery
439. (Cat. 434) *Rocky Bay with Figures*, *c.* 1830; 36 × 49; Tate Gallery
440. (Cat. 437) *Tivoli: Tobias and the Angel*, *c.* 1835; $35\frac{5}{8} \times 47\frac{5}{8}$; Tate Gallery
441. (Cat. 438) *The Arch of Constantine, Rome*, *c.* 1835; 36 × 48; Tate Gallery
442. (Cat. 435) *The Vision of Jacob's Ladder*, *c.* 1830?; $48\frac{1}{2} \times 74$; Tate Gallery
443. (Cat. 440) *Heidelberg*, *c.* 1840–5; $52 \times 79\frac{1}{2}$; Tate Gallery
444. (Cat. 439) *Mountain Glen, perhaps with Diana and Actæon*, *c.* 1835–40; $58\frac{3}{4} \times 43\frac{3}{4}$; Tate Gallery
445. (Cat. 444) *A Lady in Van Dyck Costume*, *c.* 1830–35; $47\frac{3}{4} \times 35\frac{7}{8}$; Tate Gallery
446. (Cat. 445) *Dinner in a Great Room*, *c.* 1830–35; $35\frac{3}{4} \times 48$; Tate Gallery
447. (Cat. 446) *Figures in a Building*, *c.* 1830–35; 36 × 48; Tate Gallery
448. (Cat. 447) *Music at East Cowes Castle*, *c.* 1835; $47\frac{3}{4} \times 35\frac{5}{8}$; Tate Gallery
449. (Cat. 448) *Two Women and a Letter*, *c.* 1835; 48 × 36; Tate Gallery
450. (Cat. 449) *Interior at Petworth*, *c.* 1837; $35\frac{3}{4} \times 48$; Tate Gallery
451. (Cat. 450) *A Vaulted Hall*, *c.* 1835; $29\frac{1}{2} \times 36$; Tate Gallery
452. (Cat. 451) *The Cave of Despair (?)*, *c.* 1835; 20 × 32; Tate Gallery
453. (Cat. 452) *Head of a Person asleep*, *c.* 1835; $9\frac{5}{8} \times 11\frac{7}{8}$; Tate Gallery
454. (Cat. 453) *The Evening Star*, *c.* 1830; $36\frac{1}{4} \times 48\frac{1}{4}$; reproduced by courtesy of the Trustees, The National Gallery, London
455. (Cat. 454) *Hastings*, *c.* 1830–35; $35\frac{1}{2} \times 48$; Tate Gallery
456. (Cat. 455) *Rough Sea with Wreckage*, *c.* 1830–35; $36\frac{1}{4} \times 48\frac{1}{4}$; Tate Gallery
457. (Cat. 456) *Breakers on a Flat Beach*, *c.* 1830–35; $35\frac{1}{2} \times 47\frac{5}{8}$; Tate Gallery
458. (Cat. 457) *Waves breaking against the Wind*, *c.* 1835; 23 × 35; Tate Gallery
459. (Cat. 458) *Waves breaking on a Lee Shore*, *c.* 1835; $23\frac{1}{2} \times 37\frac{1}{2}$; Tate Gallery
460. (Cat. 459) *Waves breaking on a Shore*, *c.* 1835; $18\frac{1}{4} \times 23\frac{7}{8}$; Tate Gallery
461. (Cat. 460) *Fire at Sea*, *c.* 1835; $67\frac{1}{2} \times 86\frac{3}{4}$; Tate Gallery
462. (Cat. 461) *Yacht approaching the Coast*, *c.* 1835–40; $40\frac{1}{4} \times 56$; Tate Gallery
463. (Cat. 462) *Stormy Sea with Blazing Wreck*, *c.* 1835–40; $39\frac{1}{8} \times 55\frac{3}{4}$; Tate Gallery
464. (Cat. 463) *Stormy Sea with Dolphins*, *c.* 1835–40; $35\frac{3}{4} \times 48$; Tate Gallery
465. (Cat. 464) *Margate (?) from the Sea*, *c.* 1835–40; $36\frac{1}{8} \times 48\frac{1}{4}$; reproduced by courtesy of the Trustees, The National Gallery, London
466. (Cat. 465) *Seascape*, *c.* 1835–40; $35\frac{1}{2} \times 47\frac{5}{8}$; Tate Gallery
467. (Cat. 466) *Seascape with Storm coming on*, *c.* 1840; $36 \times 47\frac{7}{8}$; Tate Gallery
468. (Cat. 467) *Seascape with Distant Coast*, *c.* 1840; 36 × 48; Tate Gallery
469. (Cat. 468) *Seascape with Buoy*, *c.* 1840; 36 × 48; Tate Gallery
470. (Cat. 469) *Sun setting over a Lake*, *c.* 1840; $35\frac{7}{8} \times 48\frac{1}{4}$; Tate Gallery
471. (Cat. 470) *A Wreck, with Fishing Boats*, *c.* 1840–45; $36 \times 48\frac{1}{8}$; Tate Gallery
472. (Cat. 471) *Rough Sea*, *c.* 1840–45; 36 × 48; Tate Gallery
473. (Cat. 472) *Seascape: Folkestone*, *c.* 1845; $34\frac{3}{4} \times 46\frac{1}{4}$; Private Collection
474. (Cat. 473) *Sunrise with Sea Monsters*, *c.* 1845; 36 × 48; Tate Gallery
475. (Cat. 474) *The Beacon Light*, *c.* 1835–40; $23\frac{1}{2} \times 36\frac{1}{2}$; National Museum of Wales
476. (Cat. 475) *Margate Harbour*, *c.* 1835–40; $18\frac{1}{16} \times 24\frac{1}{16}$; Walker Art Gallery, Liverpool
477. (Cat. 476) *Off the Nore: Wind and Water*, *c.* 1840–5; 12 × 18; Yale Center for British Art, Paul Mellon Collection
478. (Cat. 477) *Wreckers on the Coast: Sun rising through Mist*, *c.* 1835–40; $14 \times 21\frac{3}{4}$; Private Collection, Germany
479. (Cat. 478) *Morning after the Wreck*, *c.* 1835–40; 15 × 24; National Museum of Wales
480. (Cat. 479) *Off Ramsgate (?)*, *c.* 1840; $12\frac{1}{4} \times 19$; Private Collection, U.S.A.
481. (Cat. 480) *The Storm*, *c.* 1840–45; $12\frac{3}{4} \times 21\frac{1}{2}$; National Museum of Wales
482. (Cat. 481) *The Day after the Storm*, *c.* 1840–45; 12 × 21; National Museum of Wales
483. (Cat. 482) *Waves breaking on the Shore*, *c.* 1840–5; $17\frac{1}{2} \times 25$; Yale Center for British Art, Paul Mellon Collection
484. (Cat. 483) *Off Deal*, *c.* 1835; $9 \times 11\frac{15}{16}$; Nationalmuseum, Stockholm
485. (Cat. 484) *A Sailing Boat off Deal*, *c.* 1835; 9 × 12; National Museum of Wales
486. (Cat. 485) *Riders on a Beach*, *c.* 1835; 9 × 12; British Museum
487. (Cat. 486) *Shore Scene with Waves and Breakwater*, *c.* 1835; 9 × 12; British Museum
488. (Cat. 487) *Coast Scene with Buildings*, *c.* 1840–45?; $12 \times 18\frac{3}{4}$; British Museum
489. (Cat. 488) *Red Sky over a Beach*, *c.* 1840–45?;

$11\frac{15}{16} \times 18\frac{7}{8}$; British Museum
490. (Cat. 489) *Ship in a Storm*, *c.* 1840–45?; $11\frac{7}{8} \times 18\frac{3}{4}$; British Museum
491. (Cat. 490) *Calm Sea with Distant Grey Clouds*, *c.* 1840–45?; $11\frac{7}{8} \times 19$; British Museum
492. (Cat. 491) *Coast Scene with Breaking Waves*, *c.* 1840–45?; $11\frac{5}{8} \times 19\frac{1}{8}$; British Museum
493. (Cat. 492) *Sea, Sand and Sky (?)*, *c.* 1840–45?; $11\frac{3}{4} \times 18\frac{1}{8}$; British Museum
494. (Cat. 493) *Sand and Sky (?)*, *c.* 1840–45?; $11\frac{13}{16} \times 18\frac{7}{8}$; British Museum
495. (Cat. 494) *Yellow Sky?*, *c.* 1840–45?; $11\frac{7}{8} \times 18\frac{3}{4}$; British Museum
496. (Cat. 495) *Coast Scene*, *c.* 1840–45?; $10\frac{5}{8} \times 11\frac{15}{16}$; British Museum
497. (Cat. 496) *Figures on a Beach*, *c.* 1840–45?; $10\frac{3}{16} \times 11\frac{3}{4}$; British Museum
498. (Cat. 497) *Sunset seen from a Beach with a Breakwater*, *c.* 1840–45?; $9\frac{3}{4} \times 11\frac{7}{8}$; British Museum
499. (Cat. 498) *Sailing Boat in a Rough Sea*, *c.* 1840–45?; $10\frac{1}{2} \times 11\frac{15}{16}$; British Museum
500. (Cat. 499) *Two Figures on a Beach with a Boat*, *c.* 1840–45?; $9\frac{5}{8} \times 13\frac{5}{8}$; British Museum
501. (Cat. 500) *Waves Breaking on a Beach*, *c.* 1840–45?; $9\frac{3}{4} \times 13\frac{1}{2}$; British Museum
502. (Cat. 502) *Venice with the Salute*, *c.* 1840–45; $24\frac{1}{2} \times 36\frac{1}{2}$; Tate Gallery
503. (Cat. 503) *Scene in Venice*, *c.* 1840–45; $24\frac{1}{2} \times 36\frac{1}{2}$; Tate Gallery
504. (Cat. 504) *Venetian Scene*, *c.* 1840–45; $31\frac{1}{4} \times 31$; Tate Gallery
505. (Cat. 532) *A River seen from a Hill*, *c.* 1840–45; $31 \times 31\frac{1}{4}$; Tate Gallery
506. (Cat. 505) *Procession of Boats with Distant Smoke, Venice*, *c.* 1845; $35\frac{1}{2} \times 47\frac{1}{2}$; Tate Gallery
507. (Cat. 506) *Festive Lagoon Scene, Venice*, *c.* 1845; $35\frac{3}{4} \times 47\frac{3}{4}$; Tate Gallery
508. (Cat. 507) *Riva degli Schiavone, Venice: Water Fete*, *c.* 1845; $28\frac{3}{8} \times 44\frac{1}{4}$; Tate Gallery
509. (Cat. 508) *Venetian Festival*, *c.* 1845; $28\frac{1}{2} \times 44\frac{5}{8}$; Tate Gallery
510. (Cat. 501) *Venice, the Piazetta with the Ceremony of the Doge marrying the Sea*, *c.* 1835; 36×48; Tate Gallery
511. (Cat. 509) *Landscape with a River and a Bay in the Distance*, *c.* 1840–50; $37 \times 48\frac{1}{2}$; Musée du Louvre, Paris
512. (Cat. 510) *The Falls of the Clyde*, *c.* 1840–50; 35×47; the Trustees of the Lady Lever Art Gallery, Port Sunlight
513. (Cat. 511) *Landscape with Walton Bridges*, *c.* 1840–50; $34 \times 46\frac{1}{4}$; Estate of the late Mr H. S. Morgan, New York
514. (Cat. 512) *Norham Castle, Sunrise*, *c.* 1840–50; $35\frac{3}{4} \times 48$; Tate Gallery
515. (Cat. 513) *Landscape: Woman with Tambourine*, *c.* 1840–50; $34\frac{3}{4} \times 46\frac{1}{2}$; Mrs M. D. Fergusson
516. (Cat. 514) *Europa and the Bull*, *c.* 1840–50; $35\frac{7}{8} \times 47\frac{7}{8}$; Taft Museum, Cincinnati, Ohio
517. (Cat. 515) *Sunrise, a Castle in a Bay: 'Solitude'*, *c.* 1840–50; $35\frac{3}{4} \times 48$; Tate Gallery
518. (Cat. 516) *Sunrise, with a Boat between Headlands*, *c.* 1840–50; 36×48; Tate Gallery
519. (Cat. 517) *Landscape with River and Distant Mountains*, *c.* 1840–50; $36\frac{1}{4} \times 48\frac{1}{4}$; Walker Art Gallery, Liverpool
520. (Cat. 518) *The Ponte delle Torri, Spoleto*, *c.* 1840–50; 36×48; Tate Gallery
521. (Cat. 519) *Inverary Pier, Loch Fyne: Morning*, *c.* 1840–50; 36×48; Yale Center for British Art, Paul Mellon Collection
522. (Cat. 521) *Mountain Scene with Lake and Hut*, *c.* 1840–45; 28×38; Tate Gallery
523. (Cat. 522) *Mountain Landscape*, *c.* 1840–45; 28×38; Tate Gallery
524. (Cat. 520) *The Val d'Aosta*, *c.* 1840–50; 36×48; National Gallery of Victoria, Melbourne
525. (Cat. 523) *The Thames above Waterloo Bridge*, *c.* 1830–35; $35\frac{5}{8} \times 47\frac{5}{8}$; Tate Gallery
526. (Cat. 524) *Abbotsford*, 1834–6; 20×25; Indianapolis Museum of Art. Gift in memory of Evan F. Lilly with the hope that it will bring beauty and inspiration into the lives of others.
527. (Cat. 525) *Sunset*, *c.* 1830–35?; $26\frac{1}{4} \times 32\frac{1}{4}$; Tate Gallery
528. (Cat. 527) *Harbour with Town and Fortress*, *c.* 1830?; 68×88; Tate Gallery
529. (Cat. 528) *Estuary with Rocks and Buildings*, *c.* 1830–40; $68 \times 95\frac{3}{4}$; Tate Gallery
530. (Cat. 529) *Seaport in the Grand Style*, *c.* 1830–40?; $68 \times 95\frac{3}{4}$; Tate Gallery
531. (Cat. 530) *Extensive Landscape with River or Estuary and a Distant Mountain*, *c.* 1830–40?; $55\frac{1}{2} \times 99$; Tate Gallery
532. (Cat. 531) *Landscape with Water*, *c.* 1840–45; $48 \times 71\frac{3}{4}$; Tate Gallery
533. (Cat. 544) British School, Nineteenth Century, *A Fresh Breeze, Part Copy of 'Sheerness and the Isle of Sheppey'*; $15\frac{1}{2} \times 19$; Tate Gallery
534. (Cat. 542) Sir Augustus Wall Callcott, *Copy of 'Sheerness and the Isle of Sheppey'*, *c.* 1807–8; $27\frac{1}{2} \times 35\frac{1}{4}$; Tate Gallery
535. (Cat. 543) Sir Augustus Wall Callcott, *Copy of 'Sheerness and the Isle of Sheppey'*, *c.* 1807–8; $14\frac{1}{8} \times 18$; Ashmolean Museum, Oxford
536. (Cat. 548) Sir Joshua Reynolds or his Studio, *Portrait of a Lady*; $29\frac{3}{4} \times 24\frac{1}{2}$; Tate Gallery
537. (Cat. 547a) Richard Wilson or his Studio, *Ruined Church beside a River, with Castle in the Foreground*; 8×6; British Museum
538. (Cat. 545) Richard Wilson or his Studio, *Tivoli: the Cascatelle*; 29×38; Tate Gallery
539. (Cat. 546) Richard Wilson or his Studio, *Valley with a Bridge over a River*; $39\frac{3}{4} \times 53\frac{3}{4}$; Tate Gallery
540. (Cat. 547) Richard Wilson or his Studio, *Niagara Falls*; $39\frac{1}{2} \times 53\frac{3}{4}$; Tate Gallery
541. (Cat. 549) Formerly attributed to Turner, *Bath Abbey: West Front*; 42×50; present whereabouts unknown

542. (Cat. 550) Formerly attributed to Turner, *Cilgerran Castle*; $35 \times 46\frac{1}{2}$; Private Collection, England
543. (Cat. 551a) *Landscape with Distant Church*; $8\frac{7}{16} \times 10\frac{1}{2}$; British Museum
544. (Cat. 552) Formerly attributed to Turner, *The Fight on the Bridge*; $17 \times 23\frac{3}{4}$; Royal Albert Memorial Museum and Art Gallery, Exeter
545. (Cat. 553) Formerly attributed to Turner. *Old London Bridge*; $40\frac{1}{8} \times 49\frac{1}{2}$; Taft Museum, Cincinnati, Ohio
546. (Cat. 554) Formerly attributed to Turner, *Edinburgh and Calton Hill from St Anthony's Chapel*; $33\frac{1}{4} \times 44$; Henry E. Huntington Library and Art Gallery, San Marino
547. (Cat. 559) Formerly attributed to Turner, *Caernarvon Castle*; 38×55; Museu du Arte de São Paulo
548. (Cat. 551) Formerly attributed to Turner, *A Stream between High Banks*; $17\frac{3}{8} \times 12\frac{3}{4}$; Harris Museum and Art Gallery, Preston
549. (Cat. 557) Formerly attributed to Turner, *Margate Jetty*; 15×11; National Museum of Wales
550. (Cat. 555) Formerly attributed to Turner, *Off Margate*; $11\frac{1}{2} \times 17\frac{1}{2}$; National Museum of Wales
551. (Cat. 556) Formerly attributed to Turner, *Emmigrants embarking at Margate*; $17\frac{1}{16} \times 21\frac{1}{16}$; Walker Art Gallery, Liverpool
552. (Cat. 556a) *The Phantom Ship*; 18×24; Whitworth Art Gallery, University of Manchester
553. (Cat. 558) Formerly attributed to Turner, *The Shipwreck*; $46 \times 56\frac{1}{4}$; National Gallery of Canada, Ottawa
554. Sir Augustus Wall Callcott after Turner, *Fishermen becalmed previous to a Storm, Twilight*, 1799 (see Cat. 8)
555. After Turner, *Calm*, plate 44 from the *Liber Studiorum*, published April 1812; $7 \times 10\frac{1}{2}$ (see Cat. 8, 93 and 94)
556. Study for *The Army of the Medes (?)*, exh, 1801; $5\frac{1}{4} \times 7\frac{3}{4}$; British Museum, 'Dinevor' sketchbook, XL, pp. 58 verso and 59 (see Cat. 15)
557. Study for *The Army of the Medes (?)*, exh, 1801; $5\frac{1}{4} \times 7\frac{3}{4}$; British Museum, 'Dinevor' sketchbook, XL, pp. 60 verso and 61 (see Cat. 15)
558. Study for *The Army of the Medes (?)*, exh. 1801; $10\frac{3}{4} \times 17\frac{1}{8}$; British Museum, 'Calais Pier' sketchbook, LXXXI, p. 165 (see Cat. 15)
559. Study for *Fishermen upon a Lee-Shore*, exh. 1802; $17\frac{1}{8} \times 21\frac{1}{2}$; British Museum, 'Calais Pier' sketchbook, LXXXI, pp. 84 and 85 (see Cat. 16)
560. After Turner, *Rispah*, plate 46 from the *Liber Studiorum*, published April 1812; $7\frac{1}{16} \times 10\frac{3}{8}$ (see Cat. 79)
561. Reverse of *Steamer and Lightship*; Cat. 279
562. Detail of inscription from *Forum Romanum*; Cat. 233
563. Detail of inscription from *Seascape with Distant Coast*; Cat. 467
564. Turner's Signature
565. Turner's Signature
566. Willem van de Velde, the Younger, *A Rising Gale*; $51 \times 74\frac{1}{2}$; Toledo Museum of Art, Toledo, Ohio (see Cat. 14)
567. Claude, *Jacob with Laban and his Daughters*; $56\frac{1}{2} \times 99$; Petworth House (see Cat. 128)
568. Titian, *The Martyrdom of St Peter*, engraved by Martino Rota; British Museum, London (see Cat. 150)
569. Van Dyck, *The Ninth Earl of Northumberland*; 54×47; Petworth House (see Cat. 338)
570. Van Dyck, *Lucy Percy, Countess of Carlisle*; $53\frac{1}{2} \times 43$; Petworth House (see Cat. 338 and 444)
571. Van Dyck, *Ann Carr, Countess of Bedford*; $53\frac{1}{2} \times 42\frac{1}{2}$; Petworth House (see Cat. 338 and 444)
572. George Jones, *The Burning Fiery Furnace*; $35\frac{1}{2} \times 27\frac{1}{2}$; Tate Gallery (see Cat. 346)

1. (Cat. 1) *Fishermen at Sea*, exh. 1796; $36 \times 48\frac{1}{8}$; Tate Gallery

2. (Cat. 2) *Moonlight, a Study at Millbank*, exh. 1797; $12\frac{3}{8} \times 15\frac{7}{8}$; Tate Gallery

3. (Cat. 3) After *Fishermen coming ashore at Sun Set ('the Mildmay Seapiece')*, exh. 1797; plate 40 from the *Liber Studiorum*, published February 1812; $7\frac{1}{8} \times 10\frac{3}{8}$

4. (Cat. 6) *Dunstanborough Castle*, exh. 1798; $36\frac{1}{4} \times 48\frac{1}{2}$; National Gallery of Victoria, Melbourne

5. (Cat. 7) *Buttermere Lake*, exh. 1798; $36\frac{1}{8} \times 48$; Tate Gallery

6. (Cat. 5) *Morning amongst the Coniston Fells*, exh. 1798; $48\frac{3}{8} \times 35\frac{5}{16}$; Tate Gallery

7. (Cat. 12) *Dolbadern Castle*, exh. 1800; 47 × 35½; Royal Academy of Arts

8. (Cat. 9) *Harlech Castle*, exh. 1799; $34\frac{1}{4} \times 47$; Yale Center for British Art, Paul Mellon Collection

9. (Cat. 11) *Kilgarran Castle*, exh. 1799; 36 × 48; National Trust, on loan to Wordsworth House, Cockermouth

10. (Cat. 13) *The Fifth Plague of Egypt*, exh. 1800; 49 × 72; Indianapolis Museum of Art

11. (Cat. 14) *Dutch Boats in a Gale (the 'Bridgewater Seapiece')*, exh. 1801; $64 \times 87\frac{1}{2}$; Private Collection, England

12. (Cat. 16) *Fishermen upon a Lee-Shore, in Squally Weather*, exh. 1802; 36 × 48; Southampton Art Gallery

13. (Cat. 17) *The Tenth Plague of Egypt*, exh. 1802; $56\frac{1}{2} \times 93$; Tate Gallery

14. (Cat. 18) *Ships bearing up for Anchorage (the 'Egremont Seapiece')*, exh. 1802; 47 × 71; Petworth House

15. (Cat. 19) *Jason*,
exh. 1802; $35\frac{1}{2} \times 47\frac{1}{8}$;
Tate Gallery

16. (Cat. 19a) *Watermill and Stream*, *c.*1791–2; $9\frac{3}{4} \times 11\frac{13}{16}$; British Museum

17. (Cat. 22) *Limekiln at Coalbrookdale*, *c.*1797; $11\frac{3}{8} \times 15\frac{7}{8}$; Yale Center for British Art, Paul Mellon Collection

18. (Cat. 20) *Self-Portrait*, *c.*1793; $20\frac{1}{2} \times 16\frac{1}{2}$; Indianapolis Museum of Art

19. (Cat. 25) *Self-Portrait*, *c.*1798; $29\frac{1}{4} \times 23$; Tate Gallery

20. (Cat. 33) *Shipping by a Breakwater*, *c.*1798; $11\frac{7}{8} \times 7\frac{5}{8}$; Tate Gallery

21. (Cat. 23) *Interior of a Romanesque Church*, *c.*1795–1800; 24 × 19¾; Tate Gallery

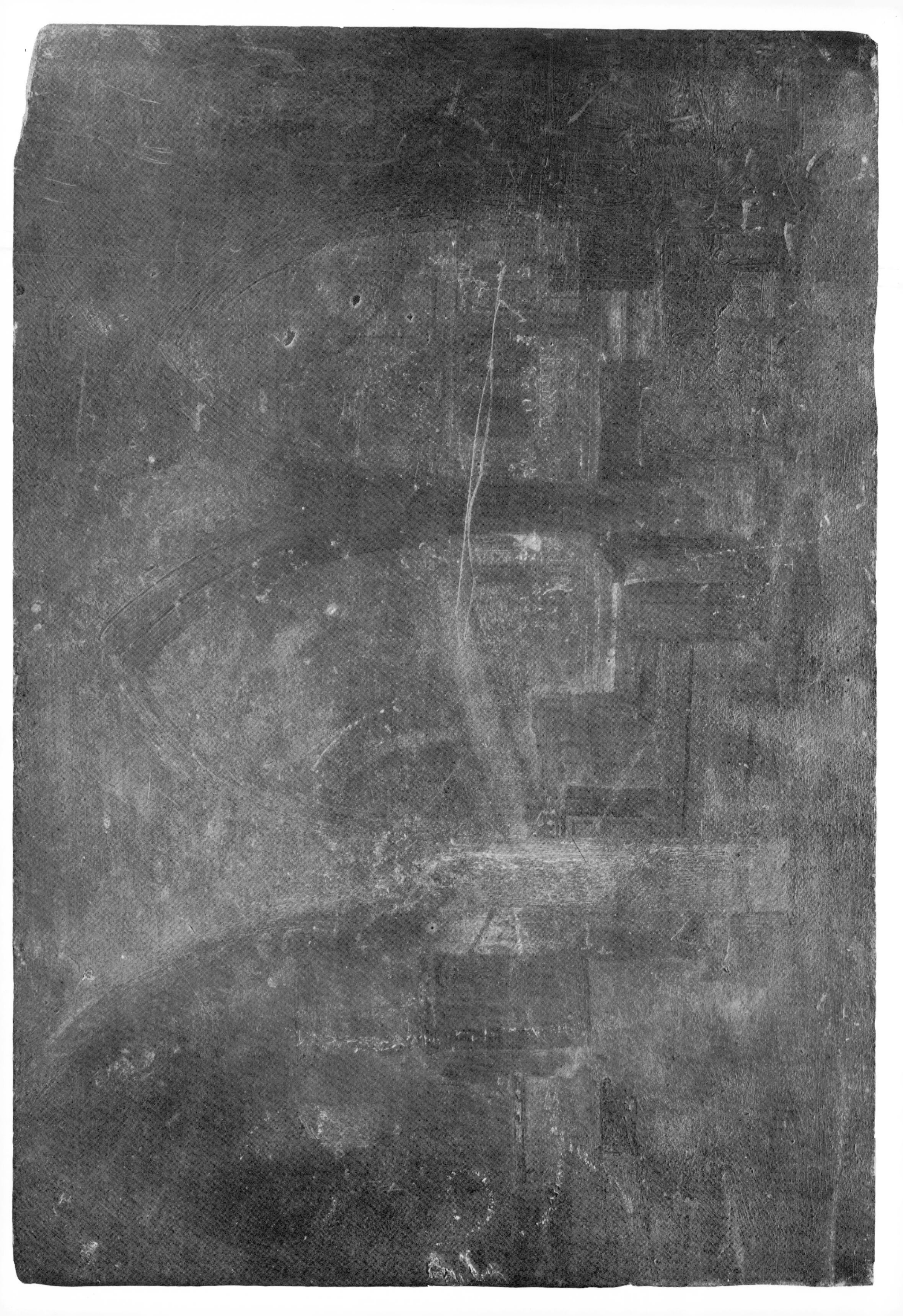

22. (Cat. 24) *(above) Interior of a Gothic Church*, *c.*1797; $10\frac{15}{16} \times 16$; Tate Gallery

23. (Cat. 28) *Caernarvon Castle*, *c.*1798; $5\frac{13}{16} \times 9\frac{1}{16}$; Tate Gallery

24. (Cat. 26) *Plompton Rocks*, *c.*1798; 48 × 54¼; the Earl of Harewood

25. (Cat. 27) *Plompton Rocks*, *c.*1798; 48 × 54¼; the Earl of Harewood

26. (Cat. 29) *View in Wales*, *c.*1799–1800; $22\frac{7}{8} \times 28\frac{5}{8}$; Tate Gallery

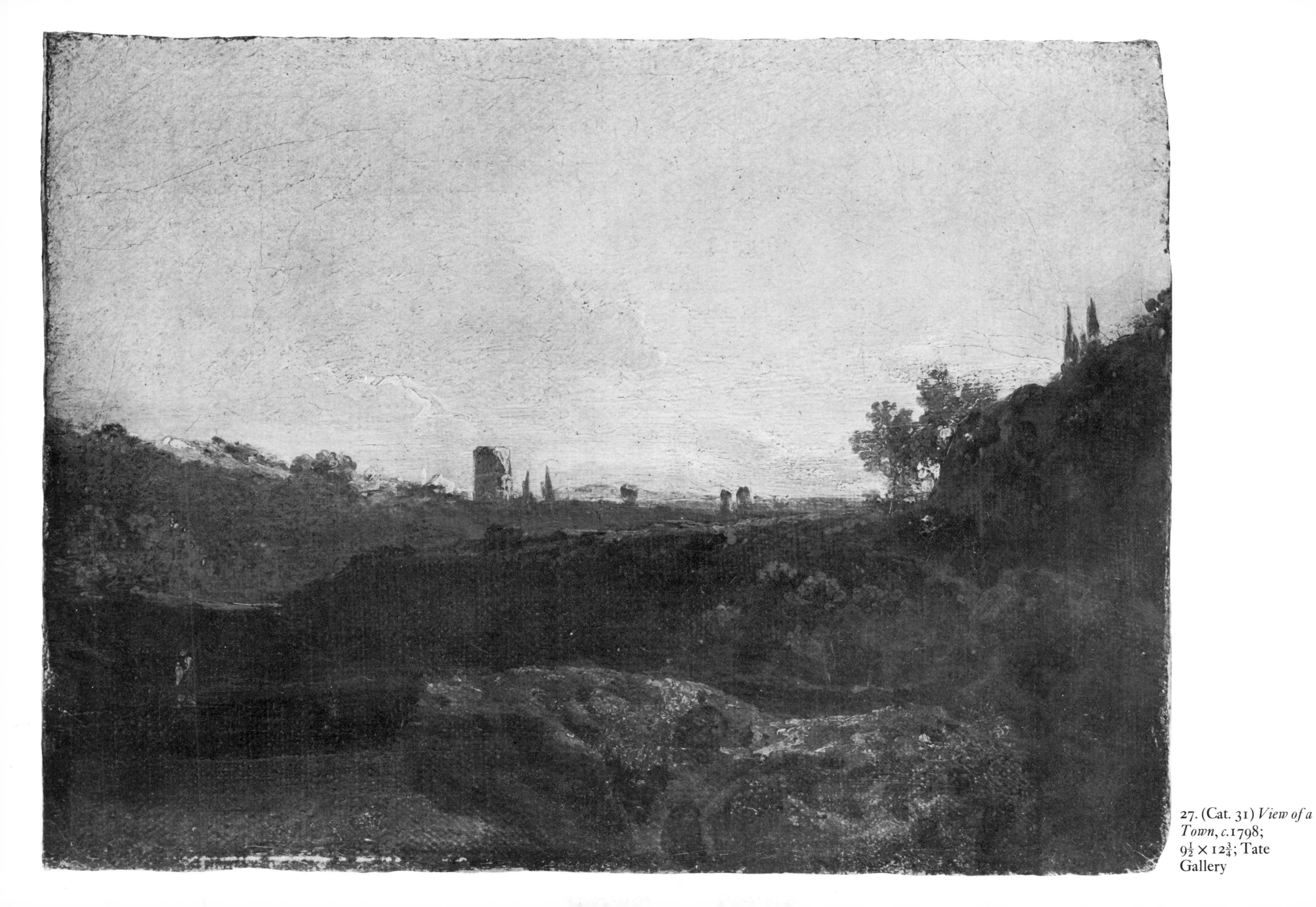

27. (Cat. 31) *View of a Town*, *c.*1798; $9\frac{1}{2} \times 12\frac{3}{4}$; Tate Gallery

28. (Cat. 32) *Dunstanborough Castle*, *c.*1798; 18½ × 26; Dunedin Public Art Gallery

29. (Cat. 33a) *A Scene on the English Coast*, *c.*1798; $9\frac{7}{8} \times 11\frac{15}{16}$; Phillips Collection, Washington, D.C.

30. (Cat. 34a) *A Dark Landscape with Trees and Mountains*, *c.*1798–9; $12\frac{1}{4} \times 15\frac{1}{4}$; British Museum

31. (Cat. 35) *Wild Landscape with Figures, Sunset*, *c.*1799–1800; $10\frac{5}{16} \times 15\frac{1}{4}$; British Museum

32. (Cat. 36) *Cilgerran Castle*, *c.*1799; 22 × 27; The Viscount Allendale

33. (Cat. 37) *Cilgerran Castle*, *c.*1798; $23\frac{3}{4} \times 29\frac{1}{4}$; The Leicestershire Museum and Art Gallery, Leicester

34. (Cat. 38) *Mountain Landscape with a Lake*, *c.*1799–1800; $25\frac{1}{4} \times 38\frac{7}{8}$; Fitzwilliam Museum, Cambridge

35. (Cat. 39) *Landscape with Lake and Fallen Tree*, *c.*1800?; $15\frac{3}{8} \times 23\frac{7}{8}$; Tate Gallery

36. (Cat. 40) *A Storm in the Mountains*, *c.*1801–2; $9\frac{1}{2} \times 12$; Lady Kleinwort

37. (Cat. 41) *Tummel Bridge, Perthshire*, *c.*1802–3; $11 \times 18\frac{1}{4}$; Yale Center for British Art, Paul Mellon Collection

38. (Cat. 42) *View on Clapham Common*, *c.*1800–2; $12\frac{5}{8} \times 17\frac{7}{16}$; Tate Gallery

39. (Cat. 35c) *A Beech Wood*, *c.*1799 or 1801; 6½ × 9½; Fogg Art Museum, Cambridge, Mass.

40. (Cat. 35a) *A Beech Wood with Gipsies round a Camp Fire*, *c.*1799 or 1801; $10\frac{3}{4} \times 7\frac{1}{2}$; Fitzwilliam Museum, Cambridge

41. (Cat. 35b) *A Beech Wood with Gipsies seated in the Middle Distance*, *c.*1799 or 1801; $10\frac{3}{4} \times 7\frac{1}{2}$; Fitzwilliam Museum, Cambridge

42. (Cat. 35d) *Knockholt Park, Kent*, *c.*1798 or 1801; $9\frac{1}{2} \times 6$; present whereabouts unknown (from old photograph)

43. (Cat. 35i) *'An Evening Effect'; Trees at Knockholt*, *c.*1801; $9\frac{1}{2} \times 6\frac{1}{2}$; British Museum

44. (Cat. 35g)
Chevening Park, Kent,
c.1801; $10\frac{3}{4} \times 14\frac{11}{16}$;
British Museum

45. (Cat. 35h)
Chevening Park, Kent,
c.1801; $10\frac{15}{16} \times 14\frac{7}{8}$;
British Museum

46. (Cat. 35e) *The Kitchen of Wells's Cottage, Knockholt*, *c.*1801; $10\frac{3}{4} \times 14\frac{3}{4}$; British Museum

47. (Cat. 35f)
Interior of a Cottage,
c.1801; $10\frac{3}{4} \times 14\frac{1}{2}$;
British Museum

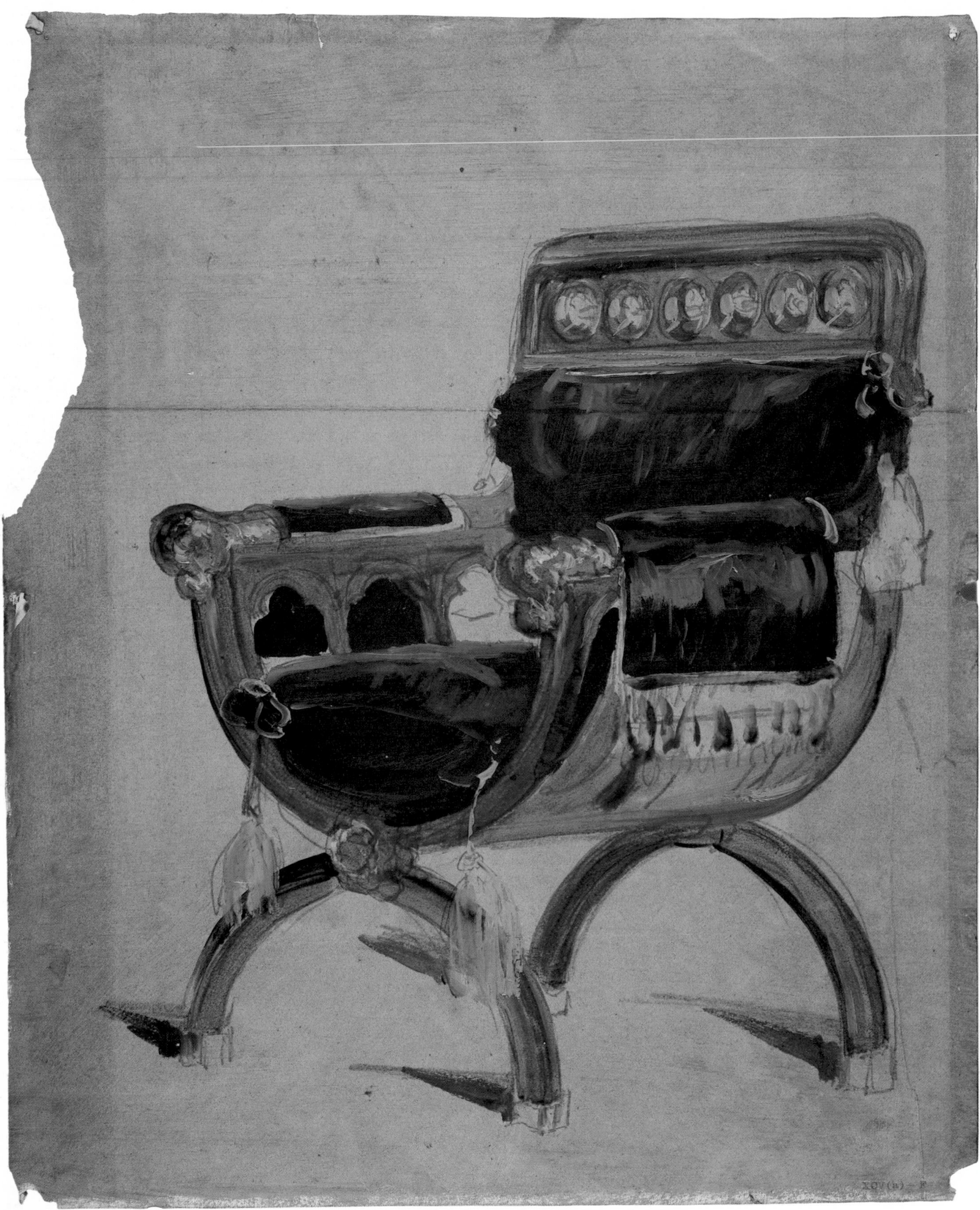

48. (Cat. 35j) *An Armchair*, *c.*1801; $8\frac{1}{2} \times 7\frac{1}{4}$; British Museum

49. (Cat. 150) *Venus and Adonis*, *c.*1803–5; 59 × 47; Private Collection, South America

50. (Cat. 34) *Æneas and the Sibyl, Lake Avernus*, *c.*1798; $30\frac{1}{8} \times 38\frac{3}{4}$; Tate Gallery

51. (Cat. 226) *Lake Avernus: Æneas and the Cumaean Sybil*, 1814–15; $28\frac{1}{4} \times 38\frac{1}{4}$; Yale Center for British Art, Paul Mellon Collection

52. (Cat. 43) *Diana and Callisto*, after Richard Wilson, *c.*1796; $22\frac{1}{4} \times 36$; Tate Gallery

53. (Cat. 44) *Tivoli: Temple of the Sibyl and the Roman Campagna*, after Richard Wilson, *c.*1798; 29 × 38; Tate Gallery

54. (Cat. 45) *Landscape with Windmill and Rainbow*, partly after Thomas Gainsborough, *c.*1795–1800; $27\frac{3}{4} \times 35\frac{1}{2}$; Tate Gallery

55. (Cat. 47) *The Festival upon the Opening of the Vintage of Macon*, exh. 1803; $57\frac{1}{2} \times 93\frac{1}{2}$; by permission of Sheffield City Art Galleries

56. (Cat. 46)
Bonneville, Savoy, with Mont Blanc, exh. 1803; 36 × 48; Newhouse Galleries, New York

57. (Cat. 124) *A View of the Castle of St Michael, near Bonneville, Savoy*, exh. 1812; $36\frac{1}{4} \times 48\frac{1}{2}$; courtesy, John G. Johnson Collection, Philadelphia

58. (Cat. 48) *Calais Pier*, exh. 1803; $67\frac{3}{4} \times 94\frac{1}{2}$; reproduced by courtesy of the Trustees, The National Gallery, London

59. (Cat. 50) *Châteaux de St. Michael, Bonneville, Savoy*, exh. 1803; 36 × 48; Yale Center for British Art, Paul Mellon Collection

60. (Cat. 49) *Holy Family*, exh. 1803; $40\frac{1}{4} \times 55\frac{3}{4}$; Tate Gallery

61. (Cat. 51) *Old Margate Pier*, exh. 1804?; $10\frac{7}{8} \times 16$; Ernest H. Gaskell, Esq.

62. (Cat. 52) *Boats carrying out Anchors and Cables to Dutch Men of War, in 1665*, exh. 1804; $40 \times 51\frac{1}{2}$; in the collection of the Corcoran Gallery of Art, Washington, D.C.

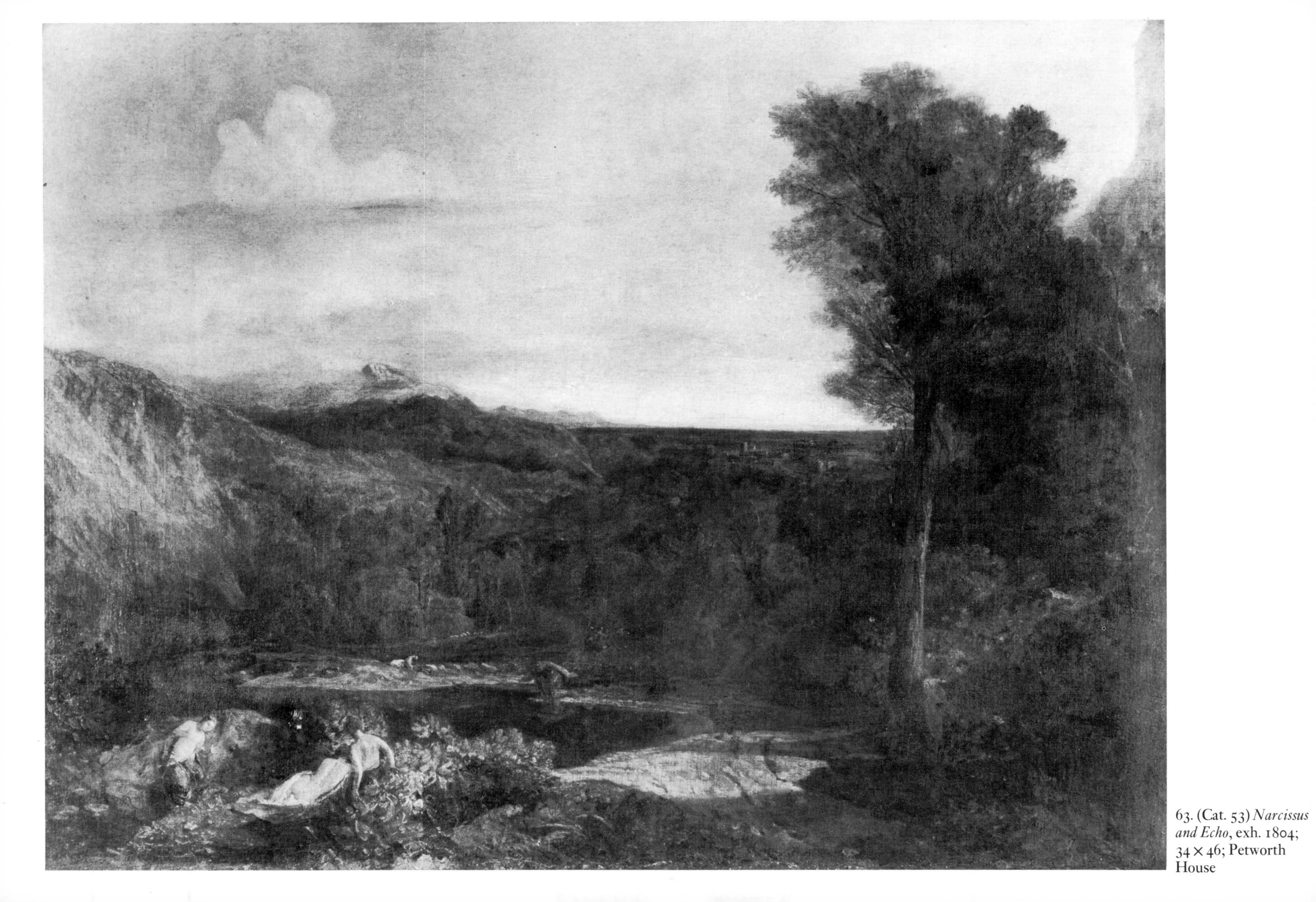

63. (Cat. 53) *Narcissus and Echo*, exh. 1804; 34 × 46; Petworth House

64. (Cat. 54) *The Shipwreck*, exh. 1805; $67\frac{1}{8} \times 95\frac{1}{8}$; Tate Gallery

65. (Cat. 55) *The Deluge*, exh. 1805?; $56\frac{1}{4} \times 92\frac{3}{4}$; Tate Gallery

66. (Cat. 56) *The Destruction of Sodom*, exh. 1805?; $57\frac{1}{2} \times 93\frac{1}{2}$; Tate Gallery

67. (Cat. 57) *The Goddess of Discord in the Garden of the Hesperides*, exh. 1806; $61\frac{1}{8} \times 86$; Tate Gallery

68. (Cat. 58) *The Battle of Trafalgar, as seen from the Mizen Starboard Shrouds of the Victory*, exh. 1806 (reworked 1808); $67\frac{1}{4} \times 94$; Tate Gallery

69. (Cat. 59) (*below*) *The Victory returning from Trafalgar*, exh. 1806?; $26\frac{3}{8} \times 39\frac{1}{2}$; Yale Center for British Art, Paul Mellon Collection

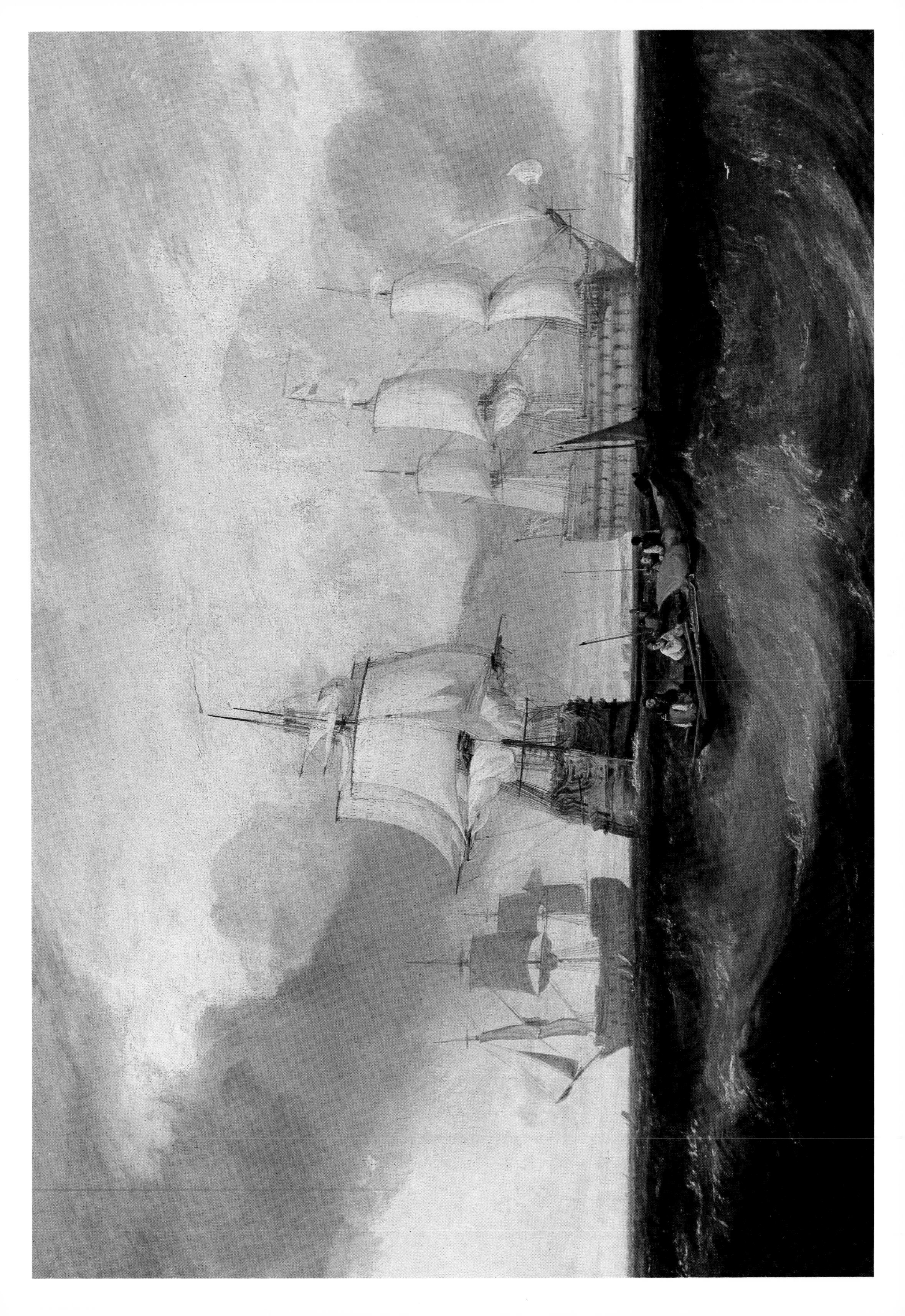

70. (Cat. 60)
Walton Bridges,
exh. 1806?;
$36\frac{1}{2} \times 48\frac{3}{4}$; the
Loyd Collection

71. (Cat. 63)
Walton Bridges,
exh. 1807?;
$36\frac{1}{4} \times 48\frac{1}{8}$;
National Gallery
of Victoria,
Melbourne

72. (Cat. 61) *Fall of the Rhine at Schaffhausen*, exh. 1806; 57 × 92; courtesy of Museum of Fine Arts, Boston

73. (Cat. 62) *Sheerness and the Isle of Sheppey, with the Junction of the Thames and Medway*, exh. 1807; $42\frac{3}{4} \times 56\frac{1}{2}$; National Gallery of Art, Washington, D.C.

74. (Cat. 64) *The Thames near Windsor*, exh. 1807?; 35 × 47; Petworth House

75. (Cat. 65)
Newark Abbey on the Wey, exh. 1807?; 36 × 48½; Yale Center for British Art, Paul Mellon Collection

76. (Cat. 66) *Cliveden on Thames*, exh. 1807?; $15\frac{1}{8} \times 23$; Tate Gallery

77. (Cat. 67) After *The Mouth of the Thames*, exh. 1807?; Mezzotint by Sir Frank Short, R.A.

78. (Cat. 68) *A Country Blacksmith disputing upon the Price of Iron*, exh. 1807; $21\frac{5}{8} \times 30\frac{5}{8}$; Tate Gallery

79. (Cat. 69) *Sun Rising through Vapour; Fishermen cleaning and selling Fish*, exh. 1807; $53 \times 70\frac{1}{2}$; reproduced by courtesy of the Trustees, The National Gallery, London

80. (Cat. 70) *Union of the Thames and Isis*, exh. 1808; $35\frac{3}{4} \times 47\frac{3}{4}$; Tate Gallery

81. (Cat. 71) *The Thames at Eton*, exh. 1808; $23\frac{1}{2} \times 35\frac{1}{2}$; Petworth House

82. (Cat. 72) *Pope's Villa at Twickenham*, exh. 1808; 36 × 47½; Trustees of the Walter Morrison Picture Settlement

83. (Cat. 73) *View of Richmond Hill and Bridge*, exh. 1808; 36 × 48; Tate Gallery

84. (Cat. 74) *Purfleet and the Essex Shore*, exh. 1808; 36 × 48; Private Collection, Belgium

85. (Cat. 75) *The Confluence of the Thames and the Medway*, exh. 1808; 35 × 47; Petworth House

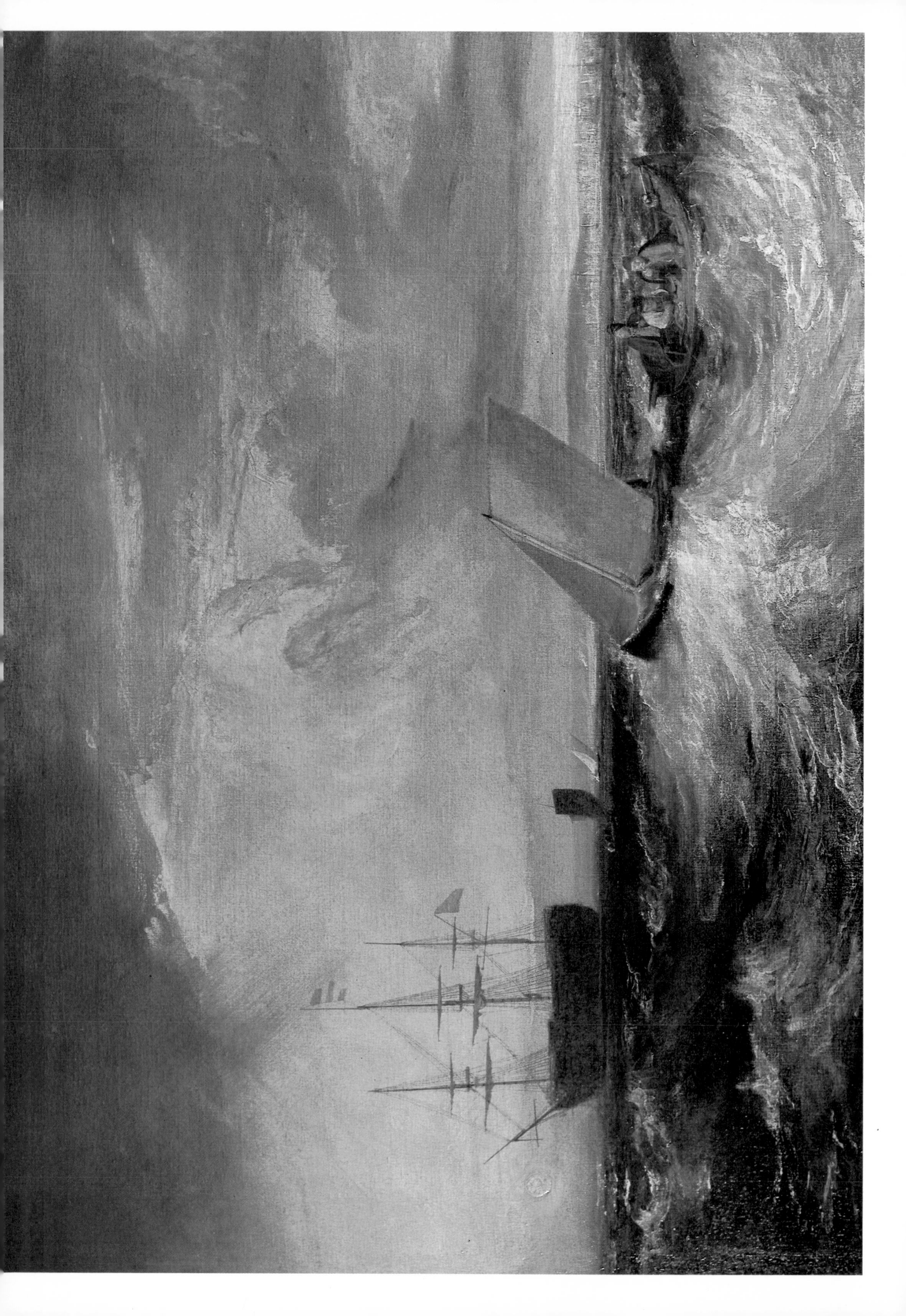

86. (Cat. 76) *(above) Sheerness as seen from the Nore*, exh. 1808; $41\frac{1}{2} \times 59$; the Loyd Collection

87. (Cat. 77) *The Forest of Bere*, exh. 1808; 35×47; Petworth House

88. (Cat. 78)
Margate, exh.
1808; $35\frac{1}{2} \times 47\frac{1}{2}$;
Petworth House

89. (Cat. 79) *A Subject from the Runic Superstitions (?)*, exh. 1808?; $36\frac{1}{4} \times 48$; Tate Gallery

90. (Cat. 80) *Spithead: Boat's Crew recovering an Anchor*, exh. 1808; $67\frac{1}{2} \times 92\frac{5}{8}$; Tate Gallery

91. (Cat. 81) *The Unpaid Bill*, exh. 1808; $23\frac{3}{8} \times 31\frac{1}{2}$; Private Collection, U.S.A.

92. (Cat. 82)
Sketch of a Bank, with Gipsies, exh. 1809?; $24\frac{1}{8} \times 33$; Tate Gallery

93. (Cat. 83) *The Quiet Ruin, Cattle in Water; a Sketch, Evening*, exh. 1809?; $24\frac{1}{8} \times 30\frac{1}{8}$; Tate Gallery

94. (Cat. 84) *River Scene with Cattle*, exh. 1809?; $50\frac{1}{2} \times 68\frac{1}{2}$; Tate Gallery

95. (Cat. 85)
Shoeburyness Fisherman hailing a Whitstable Hoy, exh. 1809; 36 × 48; National Gallery of Canada, Ottawa

96. (Cat. 86) *Thomson's Æolian Harp*, exh. 1809; $65\frac{5}{8} \times 120\frac{1}{2}$; City Art Galleries, Manchester

97. (Cat. 87)
Fishing upon the Blythe-Sand, Tide setting in, exh. 1809; 35 × 47; Tate Gallery

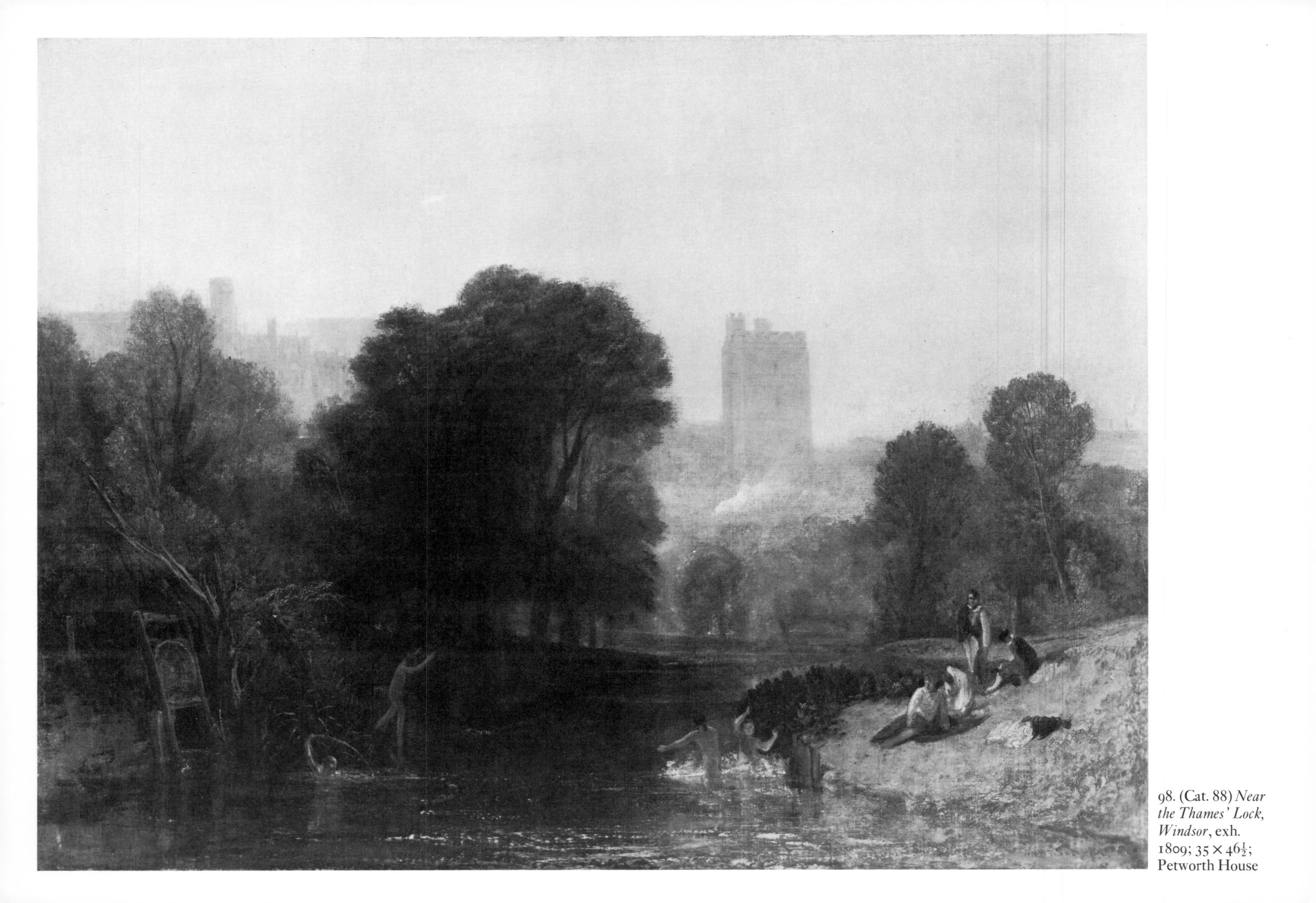

98. (Cat. 88) *Near the Thames' Lock, Windsor*, exh. 1809; 35 × 46½; Petworth House

99. (Cat. 89) *Ploughing up Turnips, near Slough*, exh. 1809; $40\frac{1}{8} \times 51\frac{1}{4}$; Tate Gallery

100. (Cat. 90) *Harvest Dinner, Kingston Bank*, exh. 1809; $35\frac{1}{2} \times 47\frac{5}{8}$; Tate Gallery

101. (Cat. 91) *Guardship at the Great Nore, Sheerness, &c.*, exh. 1809; 36 × 49; Private Collection, England

102. (Cat. 92) *Trout Fishing in the Dee*, exh. 1809; 36 × 48; Taft Museum, Cincinnati, Ohio

103. (Cat. 95) *The Sun rising through Vapour*, exh. 1809?; $27\frac{1}{2} \times 40$; the Barber Institute of Fine Arts, University of Birmingham

104. (Cat. 97)
London, exh.
1809; $35\frac{1}{2} \times 47\frac{1}{4}$;
Tate Gallery

105. (Cat. 100) *The Garreteer's Petition*, exh. 1809; $20\frac{7}{8} \times 30\frac{3}{4}$; Tate Gallery

106. (Cat. 98)
Tabley, the Seat of Sir J. F. Leicester, Bart.: Windy Day, exh. 1809;
$36 \times 47\frac{1}{2}$; Victoria University of Manchester

107. (Cat. 99) *Tabley, the Seat of Sir J. F. Leicester, Bart.: Calm Morning*, exh. 1809; 36 × 48; Petworth House

108. (Cat. 101) *Grand Junction Canal at Southall Mill*, exh. 1810; $36\frac{1}{4} \times 48$; Private Collection, London

109. (Cat. 102) *High Street, Oxford*, exh. 1810; $27 \times 39\frac{1}{2}$; the Loyd Collection

110. (Cat. 103) *Lake of Geneva, from Montreux, Chillion, &c.*, exh. 1810; $41\frac{1}{2} \times 65$; Los Angeles County Museum of Art, Adele S. Browning Memorial Collection

111. (Cat. 104) *Linlithgow Palace, Scotland*, exh. 1810; 36 × 48; Walker Art Gallery, Liverpool

112. (Cat. 105) *Fishmarket on the Sands – Hastings?*, exh. 1810; $35\frac{3}{4} \times 47\frac{1}{2}$; William Rockhill Nelson Gallery and Atkins Museum of Fine Arts, Kansas City

113. (Cat. 106) *Calder Bridge, Cumberland*, exh. 1810; 36 × 48; Professor Hamilton Emmons

114. (Cat. 107) *Dorchester Mead, Oxfordshire*, exh. 1810; 40 × 51¼; Tate Gallery

115. (Cat. 108) *Cockermouth Castle*, exh. 1810; $23\frac{3}{4} \times 35\frac{1}{2}$; Petworth House

116. (Cat. 111) *Lowther Castle, Westmorland, the Seat of the Earl of Lonsdale: Evening*, exh. 1810; $35\frac{1}{2} \times 48$; Private Collection, England

117. (Cat. 112) *Lowther Castle, Westmorland, the Seat of the Earl of Lonsdale: Mid-Day*, exh. 1810; $35\frac{1}{2} \times 48$; Private Collection, England

118. (Cat. 109) *The Fall of an Avalanche in the Grisons*, exh. 1810; $35\frac{1}{2} \times 47\frac{1}{4}$; Tate Gallery

119. (Cat. 115) *Apollo and Python*, exh. 1811; $57\frac{1}{4} \times 93\frac{1}{2}$; Tate Gallery

120. (Cat. 113)
Petworth, Sussex, the Seat of the Earl of Egremont: Dewy Morning, exh. 1810; $36 \times 47\frac{1}{2}$; Petworth House

121. (Cat. 116)
Somer-Hill, the Seat of W. F. Woodgate, Esq., exh. 1811;
$36 \times 48\frac{1}{2}$; National Gallery of Scotland
(Photo: Tom Scott)

122. (Cat. 114) *Mercury and Herse*, exh. 1811; 75 × 63; Private Collection, England

123. (Cat. 130) *Crossing the Brook*, exh. 1815; 76 × 65; Tate Gallery

124. (Cat. 117) *Whalley Bridge and Abbey, Lancashire: Dyers washing and drying Cloth*, exh. 1811; $24\frac{1}{8} \times 36\frac{3}{8}$; the Loyd Collection

125. (Cat. 121) *Saltash with the Water Ferry*, exh. 1812; $35\frac{3}{8} \times 47\frac{3}{4}$; The Metropolitan Museum of Art, New York

126. (Cat. 119) *Hulks on the Tamar*, exh. 1812?; $35\frac{1}{2} \times 47\frac{1}{2}$; Petworth House

127. (Cat. 120)
Teignmouth, exh.
1812; $35\frac{1}{2} \times 47\frac{1}{2}$;
Petworth House

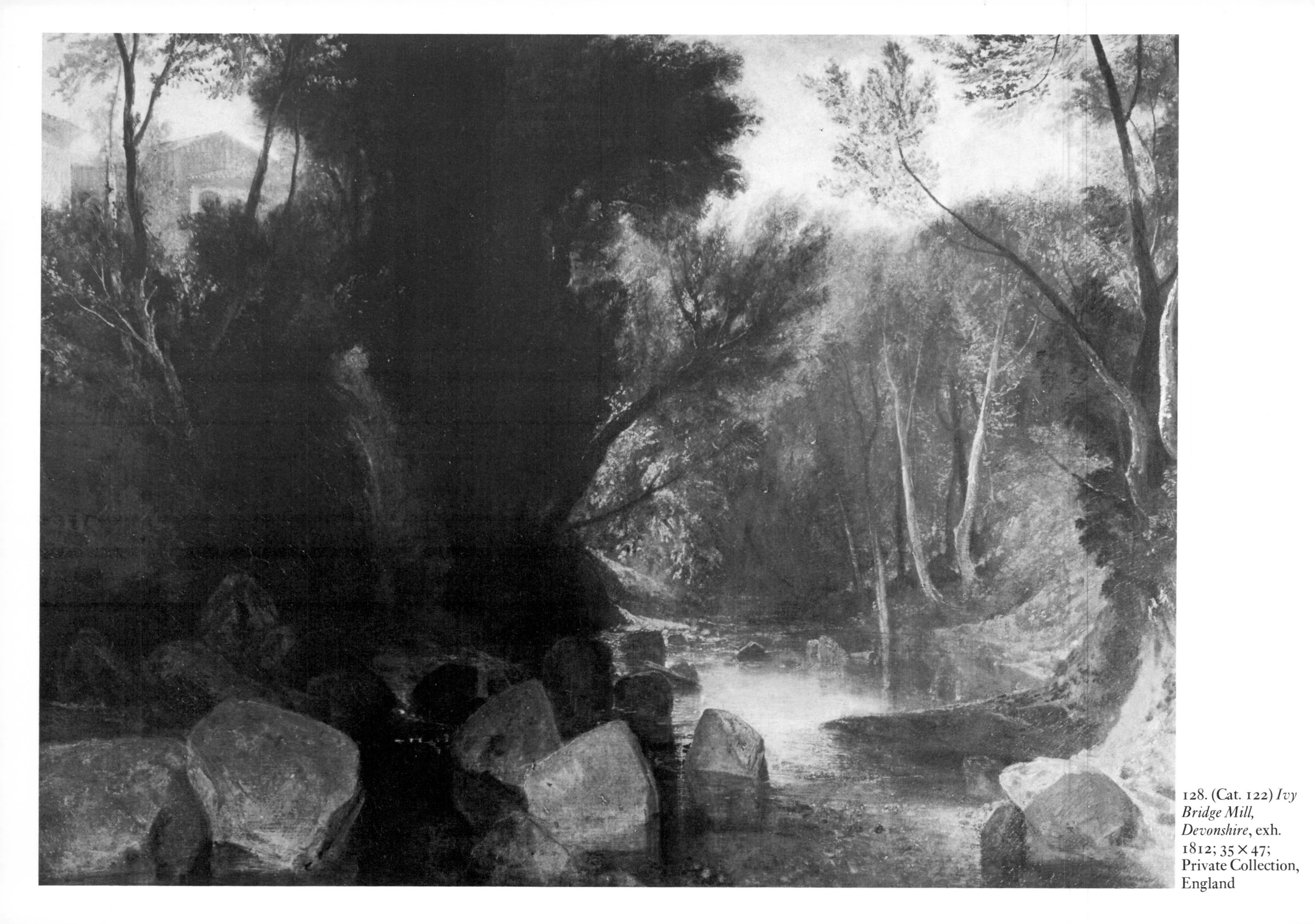

128. (Cat. 122) *Ivy Bridge Mill, Devonshire*, exh. 1812; 35 × 47; Private Collection, England

129. (Cat. 123) *St Mawes at the Pilchard Season*, exh. 1812; $35\frac{7}{8} \times 47\frac{1}{2}$; Tate Gallery

130. (Cat. 125) *Oxford from the Abingdon Road*, exh. 1812; 26 × 38½; Private Collection, England

131. (Cat. 126) *Snow Storm: Hannibal and his Army crossing the Alps*, exh. 1812; $57\frac{1}{2} \times 93\frac{1}{2}$; Tate Gallery

132. (Cat. 127) *Frosty Morning*, exh. 1813; $44\frac{3}{4} \times 68\frac{3}{4}$; Tate Gallery

133. (Cat. 131) *Dido building Carthage*, exh. 1815; $61\frac{1}{4} \times 91\frac{1}{4}$; reproduced by courtesy of the Trustees, The National Gallery, London

134. (Cat. 128) *Apullia in Search of Appulus*, exh. 1814; $57\frac{1}{2} \times 93\frac{7}{8}$; Tate Gallery

135. (Cat. 129) *Dido and Æneas*, exh. 1814; $57\frac{1}{2} \times 93\frac{3}{8}$; Tate Gallery

136. (Cat. 132) *The Eruption of the Souffrier Mountains*, exh. 1815; $31\frac{3}{4} \times 41\frac{1}{4}$; University of Liverpool

137. (Cat. 135) *The Decline of the Carthaginian Empire*, exh. 1817; 67×94; Tate Gallery

138. (Cat. 133) *The Temple of Jupiter Panellenius restored*, exh. 1816; 46 × 70; Private Collection, New York

139. (Cat. 134) *View of the Temple of Jupiter Panellenius, with the Greek National Dance of the Romaika*, exh. 1816; $46\frac{1}{4} \times 70$; the Duke of Northumberland, K.G.

140. (Cat. 137) *Dort or Dordrecht: the Dort Packet-Boat from Rotterdam becalmed*, exh. 1818; 62 × 92; Yale Center for British Art, Paul Mellon Collection

141. (Cat. 138) *The Field of Waterloo*, exh. 1818; 58 × 94; Tate Gallery

142. (Cat. 136) *Raby Castle, the Seat of the Earl of Darlington*, exh. 1818; $46\frac{7}{8} \times 71\frac{1}{8}$; Walters Art Gallery, Baltimore

143. (Cat. 139) *Entrance of the Meuse: Orange-Merchant on the Bar, going to Pieces*, exh. 1819; 69 × 97; Tate Gallery

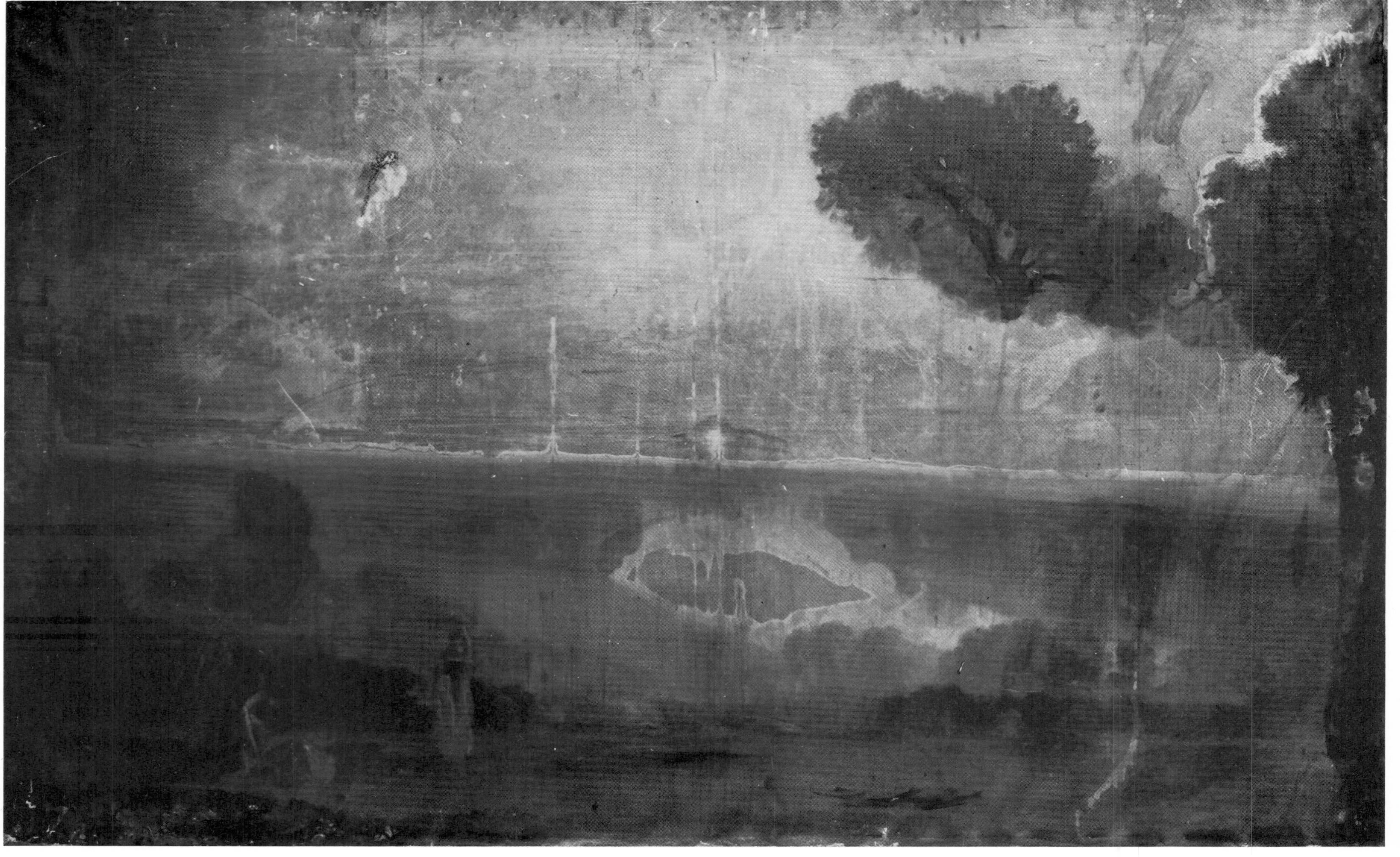

144. (Cat. 227) *Richmond Hill with Girls carrying Corn*, *c.*1819; 58 × 93¾; Tate Gallery

145. (Cat. 140) *England: Richmond Hill, on the Prince Regent's Birthday*, exh. 1819; $70\frac{7}{8} \times 131\frac{3}{4}$; Tate Gallery

146. (Cat. 141)
Conway Castle,
c.1803; $40\frac{3}{4} \times 55$;
Trustees of the
Grosvenor Estate

147. (Cat. 142)
Fishing Boats entering Calais Harbour, *c.*1803;
29 × 38$\frac{3}{4}$;
Copyright the Frick Collection, New York

148. (Cat. 143) *Seascape with a Squall coming up*, *c.*1803–4; 18 × 24; from the collection of Malden Public Library, Malden, Massachusetts

149. (Cat. 144) *A Coast Scene with Fishermen hauling a Boat ashore (the 'Iveagh Seapiece')*, *c.*1803–4; 36 × 48; The Greater London Council as Trustees of the Iveagh Bequest, Kenwood

150. (Cat. 145)
Fishmarket on the Beach, *c.*1802–4;
$17\frac{1}{2} \times 23\frac{1}{4}$;
R. F. Robertson-Glasgow, Esq.

151. (Cat. 145a) *Grenoble seen from the River Drac*, *c.*1802–3; $14\frac{1}{4} \times 25\frac{1}{4}$; Tate Gallery

152. (Cat. 145b) *Mountain Scene with Castle, probably Martigny*, *c.*1802–3; $17\frac{1}{4} \times 21\frac{1}{4}$; Tate Gallery

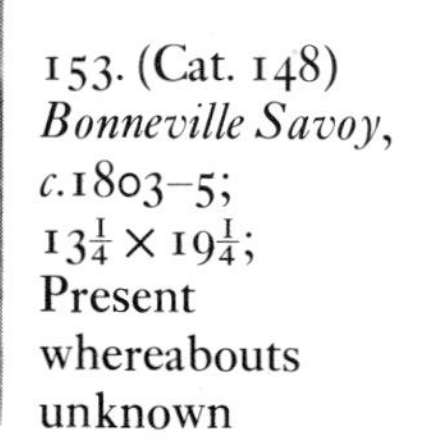

153. (Cat. 148) *Bonneville Savoy*, *c.*1803–5; $13\frac{1}{4} \times 19\frac{1}{4}$; Present whereabouts unknown

154. (Cat. 147) *The Devil's Bridge, St Gothard*, *c.*1803–4; $31\frac{3}{4} \times 24\frac{3}{4}$; Private Collection

155. (Cat. 146) *The Pass of St Gothard*, *c.*1803–4; $31\frac{3}{4} \times 25\frac{1}{4}$; City Museums and Art Gallery, Birmingham

156. (Cat. 149) *Windsor Castle from the Thames*, *c.*1805; $35\frac{3}{4} \times 48$; Petworth House

157. (Cat. 151) *Venus and the Dead Adonis*, *c.*1805?; $12\frac{1}{2} \times 17\frac{3}{4}$; Tate Gallery

158. (Cat. 152) *The Procuress?*, *c.*1805?; $47\frac{7}{8} \times 36$; Tate Gallery

159. (Cat. 153) *The Finding of Moses*, *c.*1805?; $59\frac{1}{4} \times 44$; Tate Gallery

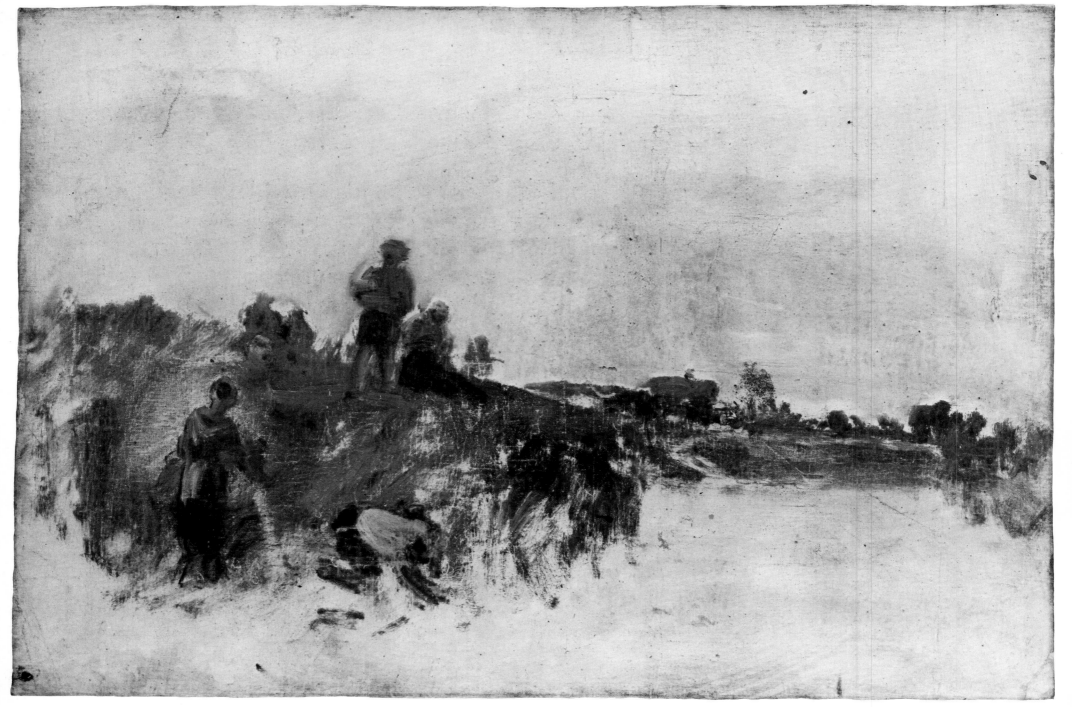

160. (Cat. 160) *Sketch for 'Harvest Dinner, Kingston Bank'*, *c.*1806–7; 24 × 36; Tate Gallery

161. (Cat. 161) *Goring Mill and Church*, *c.*1806–7; $33\frac{3}{4} \times 45\frac{3}{4}$; Tate Gallery

162. (Cat. 162)
Caversham Bridge,
*c.*1806–7;
$33\frac{5}{8} \times 45\frac{5}{8}$; Tate
Gallery

163. (Cat. 163) *A Thames Backwater with Windsor Castle in the Distance*, *c.*1806–7; $34\frac{1}{8} \times 47\frac{5}{8}$; Tate Gallery

164. (Cat. 164)
Hampton Court from the Thames, *c.*1806–7;
$33\frac{3}{4} \times 47\frac{1}{4}$; Tate Gallery

165. (Cat. 165) *The Thames glimpsed between Trees, possibly at Kew Bridge*, *c.*1806–7; $35\frac{7}{8} \times 47\frac{7}{8}$; Tate Gallery

166. (Cat. 166) *House beside the River*, *c.*1806–7; $35\frac{5}{8} \times 45\frac{7}{8}$; Tate Gallery

167. (Cat. 167) *Weir and Cattle*, *c.*1806–7; $34\frac{3}{4} \times 47\frac{1}{4}$; Tate Gallery

168. (Cat. 168) *Barge on the River, Sunset*, *c.*1806–7; $33\frac{1}{2} \times 45\frac{3}{4}$; Tate Gallery

169. (Cat. 169) *Trees beside the River, with Bridge in the Middle Distance*, *c.*1806–7; $34\frac{5}{8} \times 47\frac{1}{2}$; Tate Gallery

170. (Cat. 170) *Men with Horses crossing a River*, *c.*1806–7; $34\frac{5}{8} \times 46\frac{5}{8}$; Tate Gallery

171. (Cat. 171) *River Scene with Weir in the Middle Distance*, *c.*1806–7; $33\frac{5}{8} \times 45\frac{1}{2}$; Tate Gallery

172. (Cat. 172) *Willows beside a Stream*, *c.*1806–7; $33\frac{7}{8} \times 45\frac{3}{4}$; Tate Gallery

173. (Cat. 173)
Washing Sheep,
c.1806–7; $33\frac{1}{4} \times 45\frac{7}{8}$;
Tate Gallery

174. (Cat. 174)
Margate, Setting Sun,
*c.*1806–7; $33\frac{3}{4} \times 45\frac{3}{4}$;
Tate Gallery

175. (Cat. 175) *Shipping at the Mouth of the Thames*, *c.*1806–7; $33\frac{3}{4} \times 46$; Tate Gallery

176. (Cat. 176) *Coast Scene with Fishermen and Boats*, *c.*1806–7; $33\frac{3}{4} \times 45\frac{3}{4}$; Tate Gallery

177. (Cat. 177) *Windsor Castle from Salt Hill*, *c*.1807; $10\frac{7}{8} \times 29$; Tate Gallery

178. (Cat. 178) *Windsor from Lower Hope*, *c.*1807; $12\frac{5}{8} \times 29$; Tate Gallery

179. (Cat. 179) *Windsor Castle from the Meadows*, *c.*1807; $8\frac{3}{4} \times 21\frac{7}{8}$; Tate Gallery

180. (Cat. 180) *Windsor Castle from the River*, *c.*1807; $7\frac{7}{8} \times 14\frac{7}{16}$; Tate Gallery

181. (Cat. 181) *Eton from the River*, *c.*1807; $14\frac{1}{4} \times 26\frac{1}{8}$; Tate Gallery

182. (Cat. 182) *The Ford*, *c.*1807; $14\frac{5}{8} \times 28\frac{15}{16}$; Tate Gallery

183. (Cat. 183) *The Thames near Windsor*, *c.*1807; $7\frac{3}{8} \times 10\frac{5}{16}$; Tate Gallery

184. (Cat. 184) *The Thames near Walton Bridges*, *c.*1807; $14\frac{5}{8} \times 29$; Tate Gallery

185. (Cat. 185) *Walton Reach*, *c.*1807; $14\frac{1}{2} \times 29$; Tate Gallery

186. (Cat. 186) *Tree Tops and Sky, Guildford Castle (?), Evening*, *c.*1807; $10\frac{7}{8} \times 29$; Tate Gallery

187. (Cat. 187) *St Catherine's Hill, Guildford*, *c.*1807; 14$\frac{3}{8}$ × 29; Tate Gallery

188. (Cat. 188) *Guildford from the Banks of the Wey*, *c.*1807; 10 × 7¾; Tate Gallery

189. (Cat. 189) *A Narrow Valley*, *c.*1807; $8\frac{1}{8} \times 6\frac{1}{2}$; Tate Gallery

190. (Cat. 190) *Godalming from the South*, *c.*1807; 8 × 13¾; Tate Gallery

191. (Cat. 191) *Newark Abbey*, *c.*1807; $11\frac{5}{8} \times 13\frac{7}{8}$; Tate Gallery

192. (Cat. 192) *Newark Abbey on the Wey*, *c.*1807; $14\frac{1}{2} \times 28\frac{15}{16}$; Tate Gallery

193. (Cat. 193) *On the Thames (?)*, *c.*1807; $11\frac{5}{8} \times 13\frac{3}{4}$; Tate Gallery

194. (Cat. 194) *Sunset on the River*, *c.*1807; $6\frac{1}{16} \times 7\frac{5}{16}$; Tate Gallery

195. (Cat. 195) *Windsor Park: Cows in a Woody Landscape*, *c.*1805–7; $18\frac{3}{4} \times 28\frac{1}{4}$; Tate Gallery

196. (Cat. 196) *Cows in a Landscape with a Footbridge*, c.1805–7; $18\frac{7}{8} \times 28$; Tate Gallery

197. (Cat. 197) *Hurley House on the Thames*, *c.*1807–9; $15\frac{1}{2} \times 27$; Mrs M. V. Gairdner and others

198. (Cat. 198) *On the River Brent*, *c.*1807–9; 14¾ × 27; Private Collection

199. (Cat. 200) *Cattle in a Stream under a Bridge*, *c.*1805–7; $12\frac{3}{8} \times 15\frac{1}{2}$; Tate Gallery

200. (Cat. 201) *Newark Abbey*, *c.*1807–8; 11 × 18; the Loyd Collection

201. (Cat. 204) *The Thames at Weybridge*, *c.*1807–10; 35 × 47; Petworth House

202. (Cat. 203) *Gipsy Camp*, *c.*1807–9; 48 × 36; Tate Gallery

Blythe Sand

[illegible] Sandwich G Ships at the Nore

3 high

3

4 feet long

4.

Gravesend

Dutch Boats

3 1/4

5 feet high

5 feet

This wants lining and a weeks work

This – 16 feet long / wants Cleaning

Sir John

Queen Ann St West Decr 12 1810

Perhaps the above slight mem^m of the only four subjects I have near the size may lead your recollection in regard to their finish or class. and if I knew when you would favour me with a call. I would most certainly remain at home

Yours most truly obliged

J M W Turner

To Sir John F Leicester Bart.

Dutch Boats, now in Sir J L's Gallery in Hill St. Pretium 300 gs

203. (Cat. 206) Letter from Turner showing sketch for *Gravesend*, lower left, *c.*1810. Picture untraced.

204. (Cat. 205) After *The Leader Sea Piece*, *c.*1807–9; plate from the *Liber Studiorum*, 1809

205. (Cat. 207) *An Artists' Colourman's Workshop*, *c.*1807; 24½ × 36; Tate Gallery

206. (Cat. 208) *Tabley House*, 1808; $9 \times 11\frac{3}{4}$; British Museum

207. (Cat. 208a) *The Straw Yard*, *c.*1808; $10\frac{3}{4} \times 16\frac{1}{4}$; Private Collection, Channel Islands

208. (Cat. 209)
Harvest Home,
*c.*1809; $35\frac{5}{8} \times 47\frac{1}{2}$;
Tate Gallery

209. (Cat. 209a) *Cassiobury Park: Reaping*, *c.*1809; $35\frac{7}{16} \times 48$; Tate Gallery

210. (Cat. 211a)
English Landscape,
*c.*1810; $7\frac{9}{16} \times 10\frac{1}{2}$;
British Museum

211. (Cat. 212)
Mountain Stream, perhaps Bolton Glen, *c.*1810–15;
$17\frac{5}{8} \times 23\frac{1}{4}$; Tate Gallery

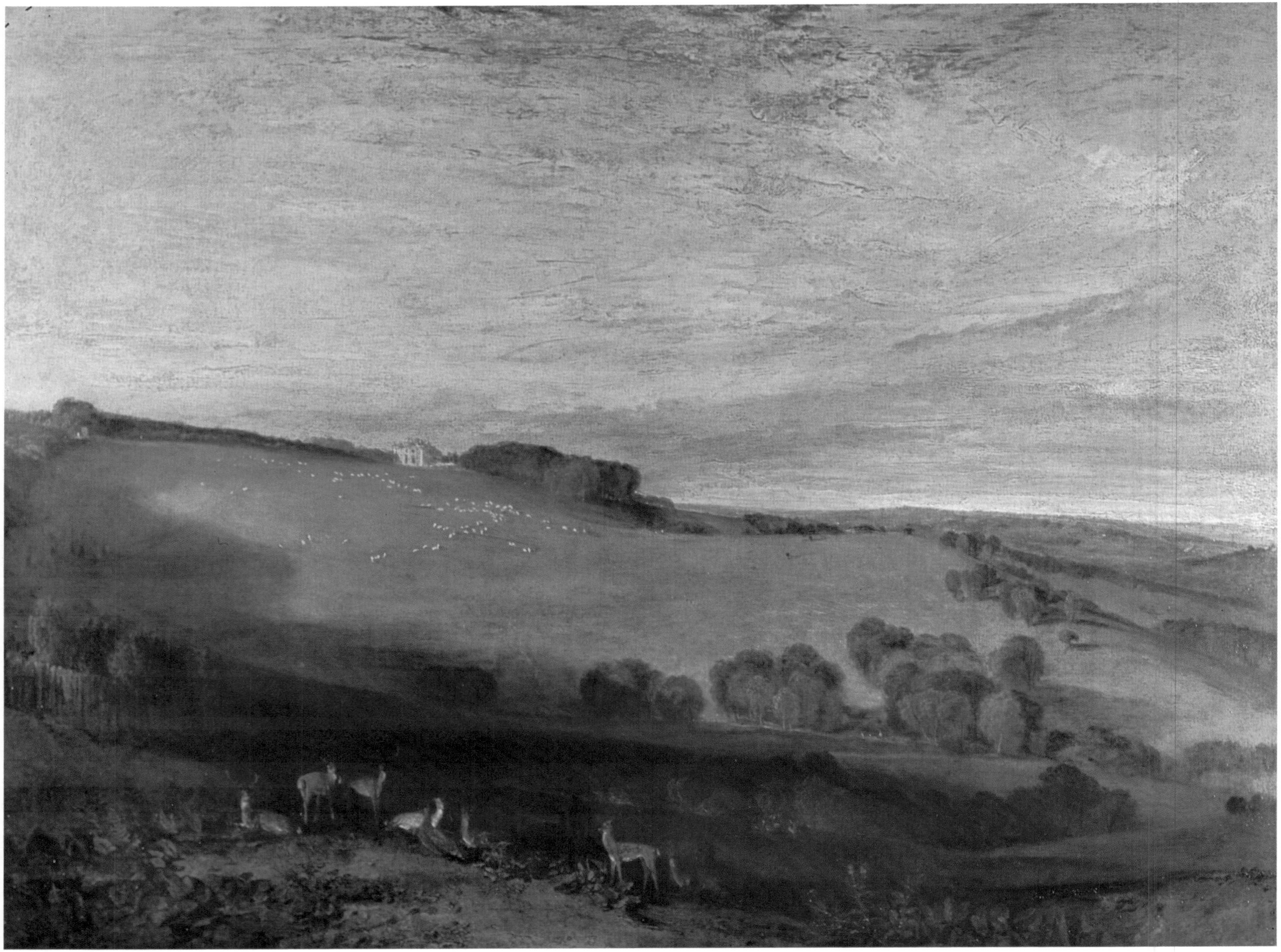

212. (Cat. 211)
Rosehill Park, Sussex, *c.*1810; 35 × 47; Lt. Col. Sir George Meyrick, Bt

213. (Cat. 210) *The Wreck of a Transport Ship*, *c.*1810; 68 × 95; Fundaçao Calouste Gulbenkian, Lisbon

214. (Cat. 213) *Milton Combe (?)*, 1813; $6 \times 9\frac{1}{4}$; British Museum

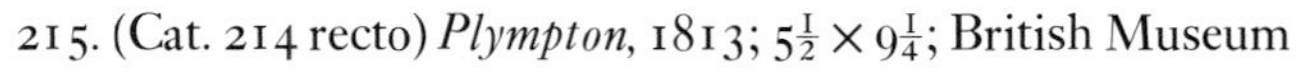
215. (Cat. 214 recto) *Plympton*, 1813; $5\frac{1}{2} \times 9\frac{1}{4}$; British Museum

216. (Cat. 215) *Hamoaze from St. John, Cornwall*, 1813; $6\frac{1}{4} \times 9\frac{1}{4}$; British Museum

217. (Cat. 216) *A Quarry, perhaps at Saltram*, 1813; $5\frac{1}{4} \times 9\frac{1}{4}$; British Museum

218. (Cat. 217) *The Plym Estuary from Boringdon Park*, 1813; $9\frac{1}{4} \times 11\frac{3}{4}$; British Museum

219. (Cat. 218) *A Bridge with a Cottage and Trees beyond*, 1813; $5\frac{7}{8} \times 9\frac{1}{4}$; British Museum

220. (Cat. 219) *Distant View of Plymouth from the North*, 1813; $5\frac{3}{4} \times 9\frac{1}{4}$; British Museum

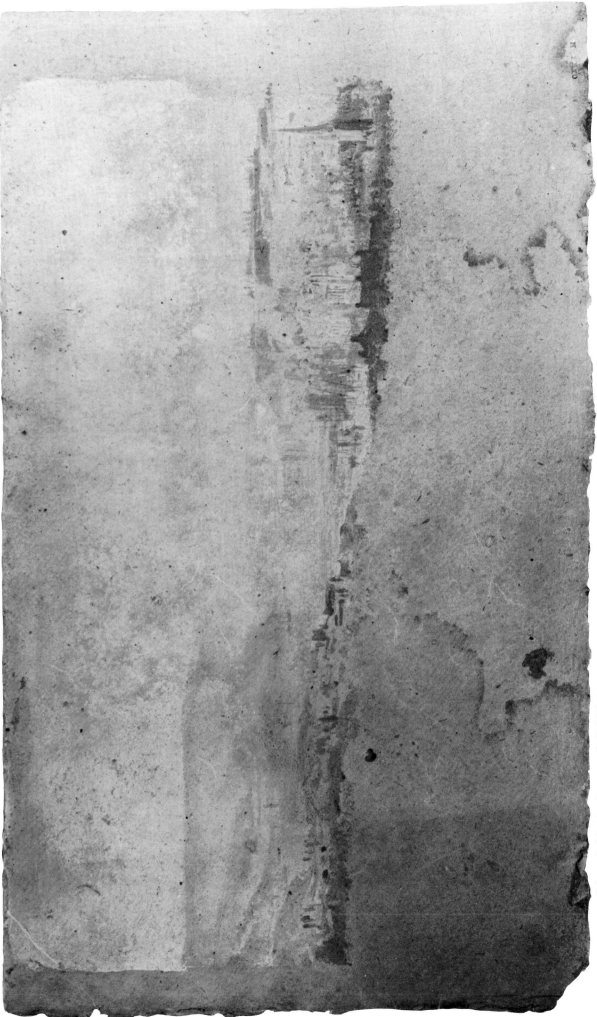

221. (Cat. 220) *Plymouth from the North*, 1813; $4 \times 9\frac{1}{4}$; British Museum

222. (Cat. 221) *Shaugh Bridge*, 1813; $6\frac{1}{4} \times 10\frac{1}{2}$; British Museum

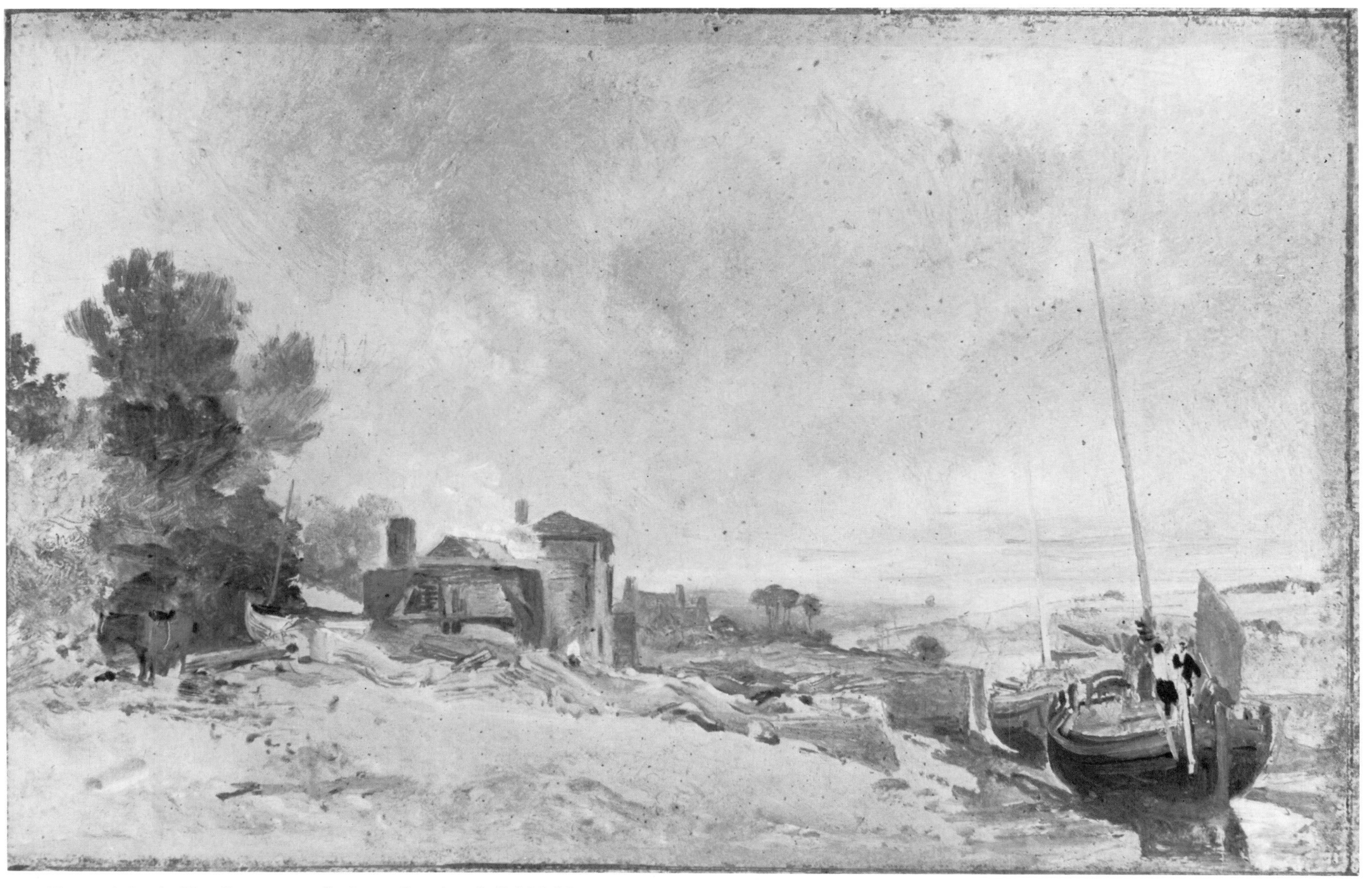

223. (Cat. 222) *On the Plym Estuary near Crabtree,* 1813; 6 × 9¼; British Museum

224. (Cat. 223) *Devonshire Bridge with Cottage*, 1813; $5\frac{15}{16} \times 9\frac{1}{4}$; British Museum

225. (Cat. 224) *The Plym Estuary looking North*, 1813; $5\frac{3}{4} \times 9\frac{1}{4}$; British Museum

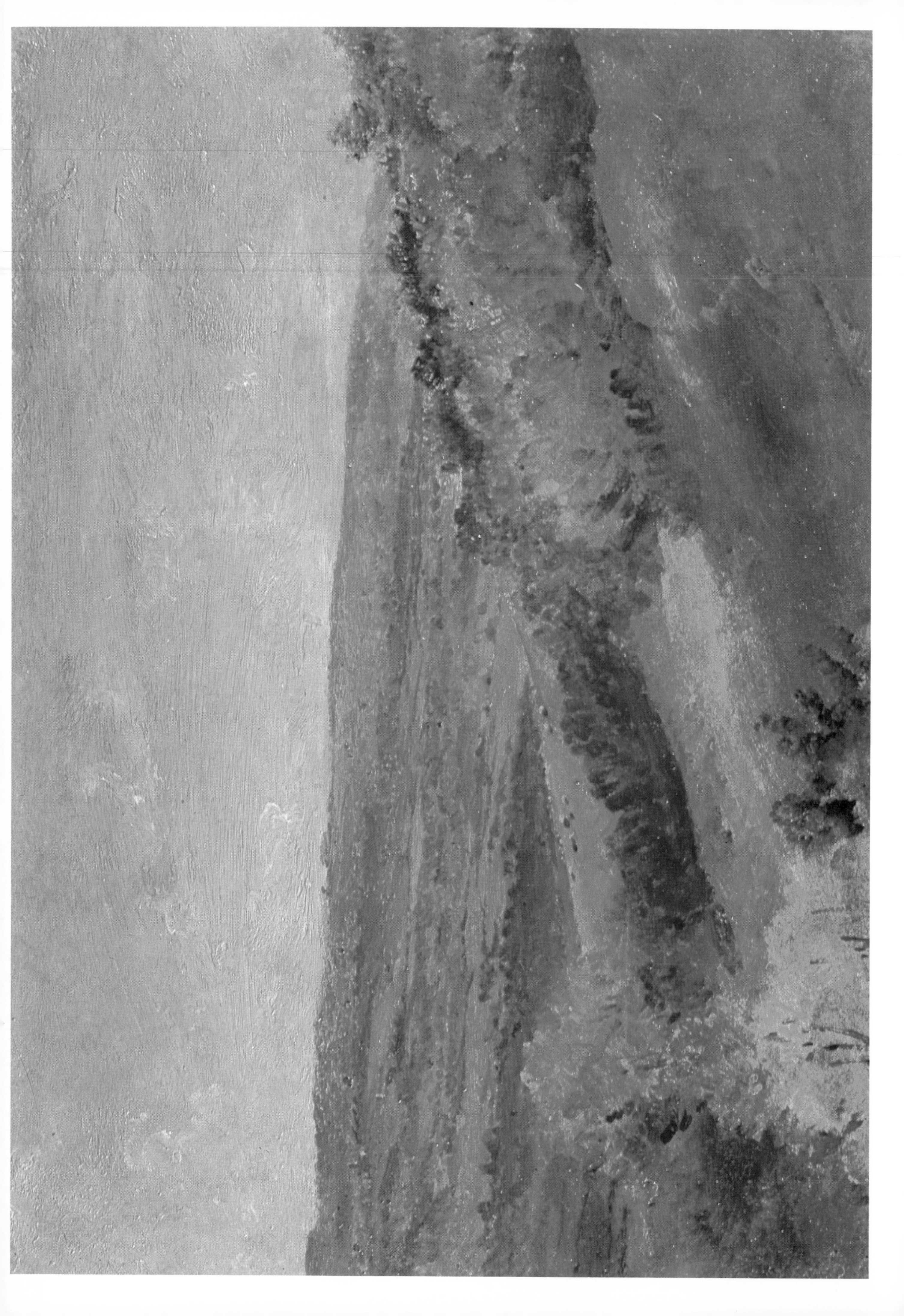

226. (Cat. 225) *(above) A Valley in Devonshire*, 1813; $7\frac{5}{8} \times 10\frac{3}{8}$; Leeds City Art Galleries

227. (Cat. 225a) *View over Plymouth Harbour*, 1813; $6 \times 9\frac{1}{4}$; Private Collection, U.S.A.

228. (Cat. 214 verso) *Landscape Study*, 1813; $6\frac{1}{2} \times 5\frac{1}{2}$; British Museum

229. (Cat. 226a) *An Evening Scene*, *c.*1815?; 3 × 5⅛; British Museum

230. (Cat. 225b) *A Devonshire Valley*, 1813; $6\frac{1}{4} \times 9\frac{3}{4}$; Private Collection, U.S.A.

231. (Cat. 228) *Rome, from the Vatican*, exh. 1820; $69\frac{3}{4} \times 132$; Tate Gallery

232. (Cat. 229) *What You Will!*, exh. 1822; $19 \times 20\frac{1}{2}$; Sir Michael Sobell

233. (Cat. 230) *The Bay of Baiae, with Apollo and the Sybil*, exh. 1823; $57\frac{1}{4} \times 94$; Tate Gallery

234. (Cat. 231) *Harbour of Dieppe (Changement de Domicile)*, exh. 1825; $68\frac{3}{8} \times 88\frac{3}{4}$; Copyright the Frick Collection, New York

235. (Cat. 232) *Cologne, the Arrival of a Packet Boat, Evening*, exh. 1826; $66\frac{3}{8} \times 88\frac{1}{4}$; Copyright the Frick Collection, New York

236. (Cat. 235) *The Seat of William Moffatt, Esq., at Mortlake. Early (Summer's) Morning*, exh. 1826; $36\frac{5}{8} \times 48\frac{1}{2}$; Copyright the Frick Collection, New York

237. (Cat. 239) *Mortlake Terrace, the Seat of William Moffatt, Esq. Summer's Evening*, exh. 1827; $36\frac{1}{4} \times 48\frac{1}{8}$; National Gallery of Art, Washington, D.C.

238. (Cat. 233) *Forum Romanum*, exh. 1826; $57\frac{3}{8} \times 93$; Tate Gallery

239. (Cat. 236) *'Now for the Painter'. Passengers going on Board*, exh. 1827; 67 × 88; City of Manchester Art Galleries

240. (Cat. 234) *View from the Terrace of a Villa at Niton*, exh. 1826; $17\frac{3}{4} \times 23\frac{1}{2}$; Mr William A. Coolidge

241. (Cat. 269)
Near Northcourt in the Isle of Wight,
c.1827; $17\frac{1}{4} \times 24\frac{1}{8}$;
Musée de Québec

242. (Cat. 237) *Port Ruysdael*, exh. 1827; $36\frac{1}{4} \times 48\frac{1}{4}$; Yale Center for British Art, Paul Mellon Collection

243. (Cat. 241) *Dido directing the Equipment of the Fleet*, exh. 1828; 59 × 89; Tate Gallery (from pre-1917 photograph)

244. (Cat. 238) *Rembrandt's Daughter*, exh. 1827; 48 × 34; Courtesy of the Fogg Art Museum, Harvard University, Cambridge, Mass.

245. (Cat. 244) *Boccaccio relating the Tale of the Birdcage*, exh. 1828; 48 × 35⅝; Tate Gallery

246. (Cat. 242) *East Cowes Castle, the Seat of J. Nash, Esq.; the Regatta beating to Windward*, exh. 1828; $35\frac{1}{2} \times 47\frac{1}{2}$; Indianapolis Museum of Art

247. (Cat. 243) *East Cowes Castle, the Seat of J. Nash, Esq.; the Regatta starting for their Moorings*, exh. 1828; 36 × 48½; by courtesy of the Victoria and Albert Museum

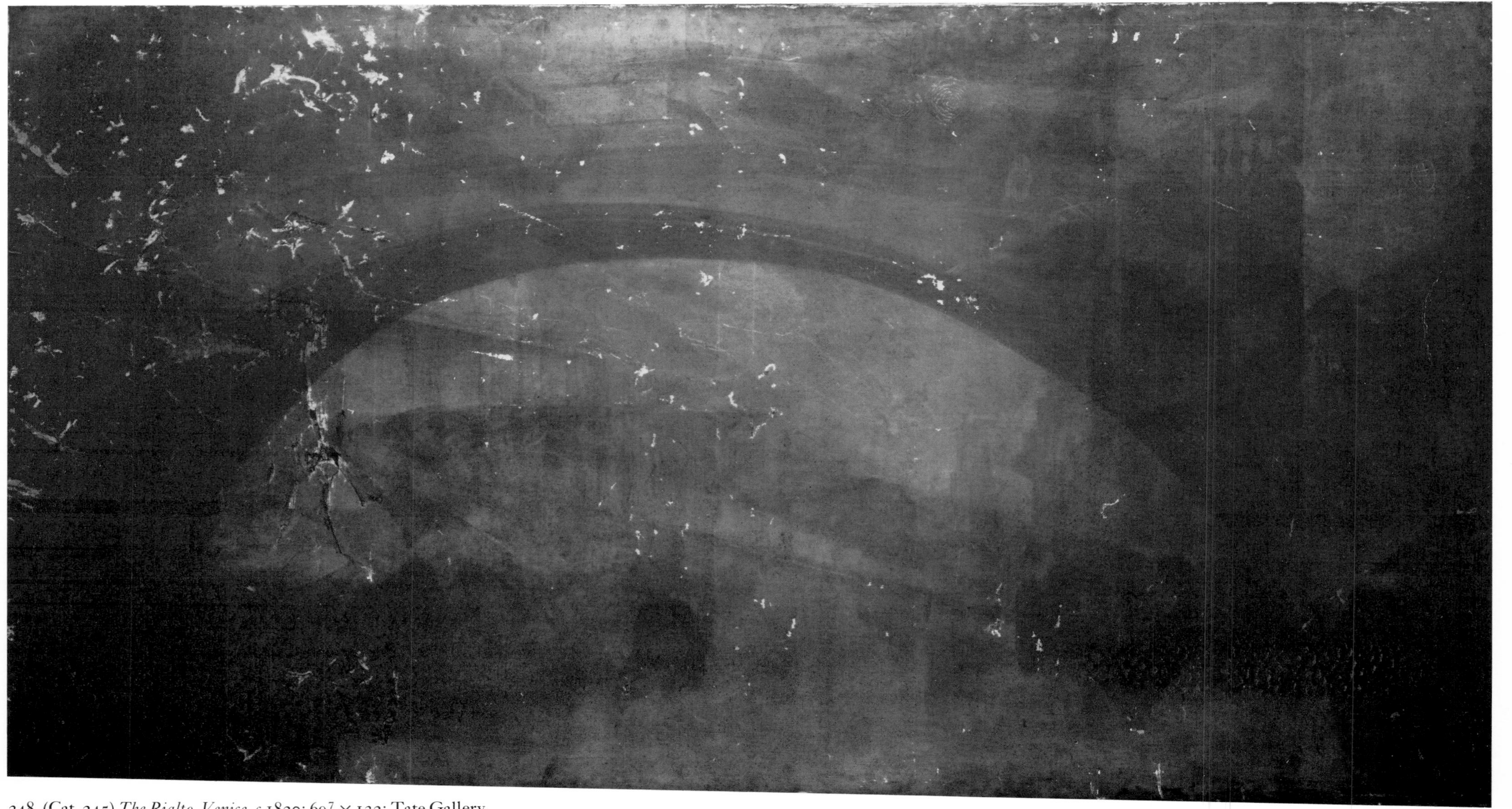

248. (Cat. 245) *The Rialto, Venice*, *c.*1820; $69\frac{7}{8} \times 132$; Tate Gallery

249. (Cat. 246) *An Avenue of Trees*, *c.*1822?; $19\frac{1}{2} \times 21\frac{1}{8}$; Tate Gallery

250. (Cat. 247) *George IV at St Giles's, Edinburgh*, *c.*1822; $29\frac{11}{16} \times 36\frac{1}{8}$; Tate Gallery

251. (Cat. 248) *George IV at the Provost's Banquet, Edinburgh, c.*1822; 27 × 36$\frac{1}{8}$; Tate Gallery

252. (Cat. 248a)
Sir Walter Scott going out to meet George IV, *c.*1822; $26\frac{3}{4} \times 36\frac{1}{8}$; Tate Gallery

253. (Cat. 248b) *George IV's Departure from the 'Royal George'*, *c.*1822; $29\frac{5}{8} \times 36\frac{3}{16}$; Tate Gallery

254. (Cat. 249)
Scene in a Church or Vaulted Hall, *c.*1820–30; $29\frac{1}{2} \times 39$; Tate Gallery

255. (Cat. 252) *The Battle of Trafalgar*, 1822–4; 102 × 144; National Maritime Museum, Greenwich

256. (Cat. 250)
First Sketch for 'The Battle of Trafalgar',
*c.*1822–3; $35\frac{3}{4} \times 47\frac{1}{2}$;
Tate Gallery

257. (Cat. 251)
Second Sketch for 'The Battle of Trafalgar',
*c.*1822–3; $35\frac{1}{2} \times 47\frac{3}{4}$;
Tate Gallery

258. (Cat. 253) *Tynemouth Priory*, *c.*1820–25?; $12\frac{1}{2} \times 24$; Tate Gallery

259. (Cat. 254) *View on the Avon*, *c.*1825; $15 \times 20\frac{7}{8}$; Private Collection, England

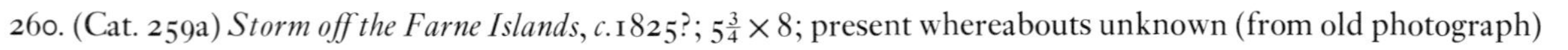

260. (Cat. 259a) *Storm off the Farne Islands*, *c.*1825?; $5\frac{3}{4} \times 8$; present whereabouts unknown (from old photograph)

261. (Cat. 256) *Valley with a Distant Bridge and Tower*, *c.*1825; $35\frac{7}{8} \times 48\frac{1}{8}$; Tate Gallery

262. (Cat. 257) *Landscape Composition*, *c.*1820–30; $21\frac{5}{8} \times 29\frac{1}{2}$; Tate Gallery

263. (Cat. 258) *The Cobbler's Home*, *c.*1825; $23\frac{1}{2} \times 31\frac{1}{2}$; Tate Gallery

264. (Cat. 259) *Death on a Pale Horse (?)*, *c.*1825–30; $23\frac{1}{2} \times 29\frac{3}{4}$; Tate Gallery

265. (Cat. 260) *Sketch for 'East Cowes Castle, the Regatta beating to Windward' no. 1*, 1827; $11\frac{3}{4} \times 19\frac{1}{4}$; Tate Gallery

266. (Cat. 261) *Sketch for 'East Cowes Castle, the Regatta beating to Windward' no. 2*, 1827; $17\frac{3}{4} \times 23\frac{7}{8}$; Tate Gallery

267. (Cat. 262) *Sketch for 'East Cowes Castle, the Regatta beating to Windward' no. 3*, 1827; $18\frac{1}{4} \times 28\frac{1}{2}$; Tate Gallery

268. (Cat. 263) *Sketch for 'East Cowes Castle, the Regatta starting for their Moorings' no. 1*, 1827; $18\frac{1}{8} \times 23\frac{7}{8}$; Tate Gallery

269. (Cat. 264) *Sketch for 'East Cowes Castle, the Regatta starting for their Moorings' no. 2*, 1827; $17\frac{1}{2} \times 29$; Tate Gallery

270. (Cat. 265) *Sketch for 'East Cowes Castle, the Regatta starting for their Moorings' no. 3*, 1827; $17\frac{3}{4} \times 24$; Tate Gallery

271. (Cat. 266) *Between Decks*, 1827; $12 \times 19\frac{1}{8}$; Tate Gallery

272. (Cat. 267)
Shipping off East Cowes Headland, 1827; $18\frac{1}{8} \times 23\frac{3}{4}$; Tate Gallery

273. (Cat. 268) *Study of Sea and Sky, Isle of Wight*, 1827; 12 × 19$\frac{1}{8}$; Tate Gallery

274. (Cat. 272) *A Sandy Beach*, *c.*1825–30; $25\frac{5}{8} \times 36$; Tate Gallery

275. (Cat. 273) *Rocky Coast*, *c.*1825–30; $19\frac{3}{4} \times 25\frac{7}{8}$; Tate Gallery

276. (Cat. 274
Seascape with Yacht (?),
*c.*1825–30;
$19\frac{3}{4} \times 26$; Tat
Gallery

277. (Cat. 275) *Seascape with Sailing Boat and a Ship*, *c.*1825–30; $18\frac{3}{8} \times 24$; Tate Gallery

278. (Cat. 276)
Lake or River with Trees on the Right, *c.*1825–30; $16\frac{1}{4} \times 23\frac{1}{2}$; Tate Gallery

279. (Cat. 279) *Steamer and Lightship*, *c.*1825–30; 36 × 47⅞; Tate Gallery

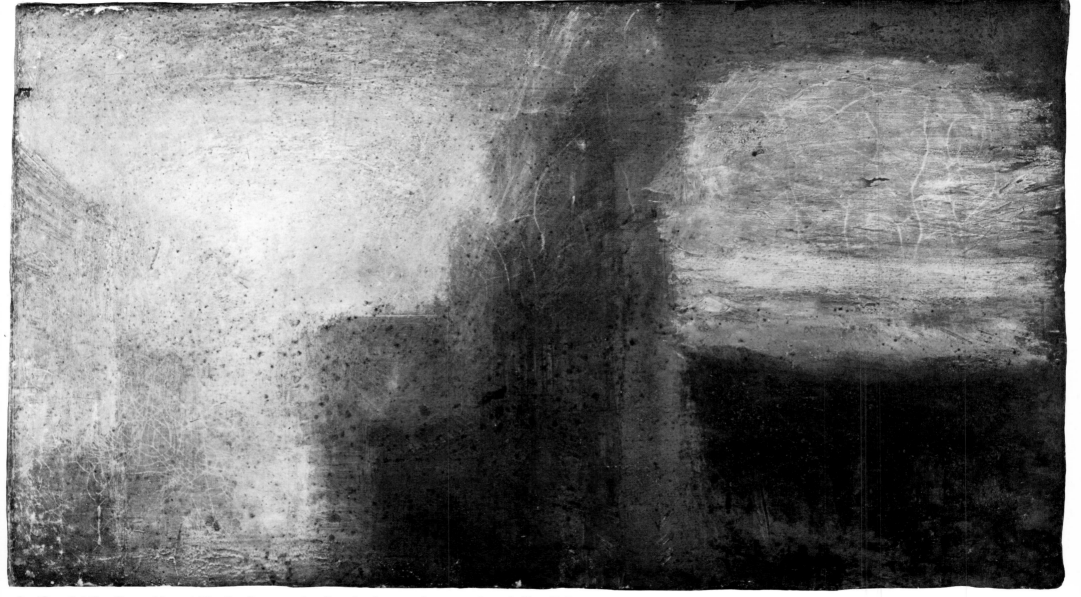

280. (Cat. 280) *Two Compositions: A Claudian Seaport and an Open Landscape*, *c.*1825–30; 13¼ × 23¾; Tate Gallery

281. (Cat. 328) *Italian Landscape with a Tower*, *c.*1825–30; 23 × 30; Tate Gallery

282. (Cat. 271) *Three Seascapes*, *c.*1827; $35\frac{3}{4} \times 23\frac{3}{4}$; Tate Gallery

283. (Cat. 441) *Studies for 'Dawn of Christianity'*, *c.*1841; $52\frac{5}{8} \times 25\frac{5}{8}$; Tate Gallery

284. (Cat. 282) *Evening Landscape, probably Chichester Canal*, *c*.1825–8; $25\frac{1}{2} \times 49\frac{1}{2}$; Tate Gallery

285. (Cat. 283) *Petworth Park: Tillington Church in the Distance*, *c.*1828; $25\frac{3}{8} \times 57\frac{3}{8}$; Tate Gallery

286. (Cat. 284) *The Lake, Petworth, Sunset*, *c.*1828; $25\frac{1}{2} \times 55\frac{1}{2}$; Tate Gallery

287. (Cat. 285) *Chichester Canal*, *c.*1828; $25\frac{3}{4} \times 53$; Tate Gallery

288. (Cat. 286) *The Chain Pier, Brighton*, *c.*1828; 28 × 53$\frac{3}{4}$; Tate Gallery

289. (Cat. 287) *A Ship aground*, *c.*1828; $27\frac{1}{2} \times 53\frac{1}{2}$; Tate Gallery

290. (Cat. 288) *The Lake, Petworth: Sunset, Fighting Bucks*, *c.*1829; $24\frac{1}{2} \times 57\frac{1}{2}$; Petworth House

291. (Cat. 289) *The Lake, Petworth: Sunset, a Stag drinking*, *c*.1829; 25 × 52; Petworth House

292. (Cat. 290) *Chichester Canal*, *c.*1829; 25 × 52; Petworth House

293. (Cat. 291) *Brighton from the Sea*, *c.*1829; 25 × 52; Petworth House

294. (Cat. 292) *View of Orvieto*, 1828 (reworked 1830); $36 \times 48\frac{1}{2}$; Tate Gallery

295. (Cat. 293) *Vision of Medea*, 1828; $68\frac{3}{8} \times 98$; Tate Gallery

296. (Cat. 294)
Regulus, 1828
(reworked 1837);
$35\frac{1}{4} \times 48\frac{3}{4}$; Tate
Gallery

297. (Cat. 295) *Palestrina – Composition*, 1828; $55\frac{1}{4} \times 98$; Tate Gallery

298. (Cat. 296) *Reclining Venus*, 1828; 69 × 98; Tate Gallery

299. (Cat. 297) *Two Recumbent Nude Figures*, 1828; $68\frac{3}{4} \times 98\frac{1}{8}$; Tate Gallery

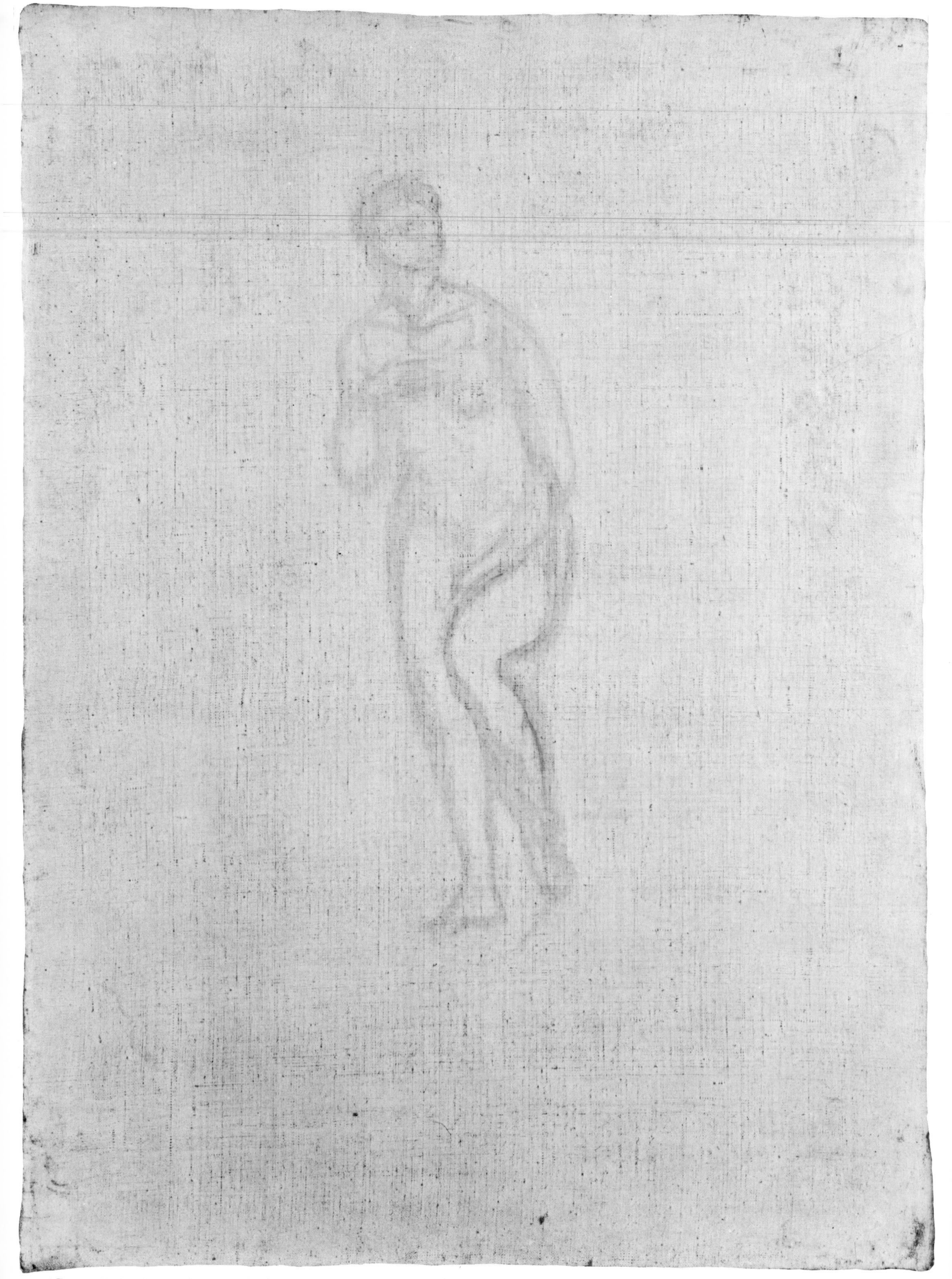

300. (Cat. 298) *Outline of the Venus Pudica*, 1828; $53\frac{3}{8} \times 38\frac{5}{8}$; Tate Gallery

301. (Cat. 281) *Landscape with a Castle on a Promontory*, *c.*1820–30?; $19\frac{1}{4} \times 15\frac{7}{8}$; Tate Gallery

302. (Cat. 299) *Southern Landscape*, 1828; $69\frac{1}{2} \times 99\frac{1}{8}$; Tate Gallery

303. (Cat. 300) *Southern Landscape with an Aqueduct and Waterfall*, 1828; $59\frac{1}{8} \times 98\frac{1}{8}$; Tate Gallery

304. (Cat. 301) *Italian Landscape, probably Civita di Bagnoregio*, 1828; 59 × 98¼; Tate Gallery

305. (Cat. 302) *Sketch for 'Ulysses deriding Polyphemus'*, 1828; $23\frac{5}{8} \times 35\frac{1}{8}$; Tate Gallery

306. (Cat. 303) *Italian Bay*, 1828; $23\frac{3}{4} \times 40\frac{1}{4}$; Tate Gallery

307. (Cat. 304) *Lake Nemi*, 1828; $23\frac{3}{4} \times 39\frac{1}{4}$; Tate Gallery

308. (Cat. 305)
Ariccia (?): Sunset,
1828; $23\frac{7}{8} \times 31\frac{1}{4}$;
Tate Gallery

309. (Cat. 306) *Overlooking the Coast, with Classical Buildings*, 1828; $23\frac{3}{4} \times 33\frac{1}{4}$; Tate Gallery

310. (Cat. 307) *Italian Landscape with Tower, Trees and Figures*, 1828; $23\frac{5}{8} \times 34\frac{7}{8}$; Tate Gallery

311. (Cat. 308) *Classical Harbour Scene*, 1828; $23\frac{3}{4} \times 40\frac{1}{8}$; Tate Gallery

312. (Cat. 309) *Rocky Bay*, 1828; $23\frac{3}{4} \times 36\frac{1}{4}$; Tate Gallery

313. (Cat. 310)
Archway with Trees by the Sea, 1828;
$23\frac{5}{8} \times 34\frac{1}{4}$; Tate Gallery

314. (Cat. 311) *Tivoli, the Cascatelle*, 1828; $23\frac{7}{8} \times 30\frac{5}{8}$; Tate Gallery

315. (Cat. 312) *Italian Landscape with Bridge and Tower*, 1828; $23\frac{3}{4} \times 38\frac{5}{8}$; Tate Gallery

316. (Cat. 313) *Claudian Harbour Scene*, 1828; $23\frac{5}{8} \times 36\frac{7}{8}$; Tate Gallery

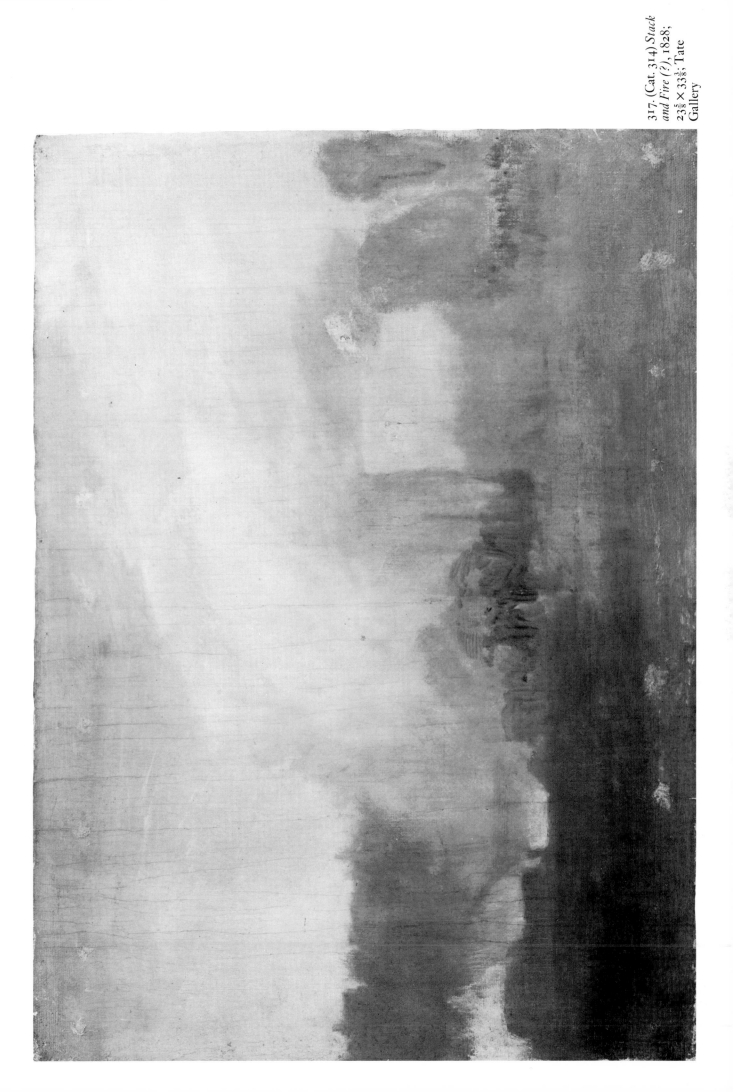

317. (Cat. 314) *Stack and Fire (?)*, 1828; $23\frac{5}{8} \times 33\frac{3}{8}$; Tate Gallery

318. (Cat. 315) *A Park*, 1828; $23\frac{3}{4} \times 38\frac{7}{8}$; Tate Gallery

319. (Cat. 316) *Scene on the Banks of a River*, 1828; $23\frac{3}{4} \times 35\frac{1}{8}$; Tate Gallery

320. (Cat. 317) *Fishing Boat in a Mist*, 1828; $23\frac{3}{4} \times 35\frac{3}{4}$; Tate Gallery

321. (Cat. 318) *Hilltown on the Edge of the Campagna*, 1828?; $16\frac{1}{8} \times 23\frac{3}{8}$; Tate Gallery

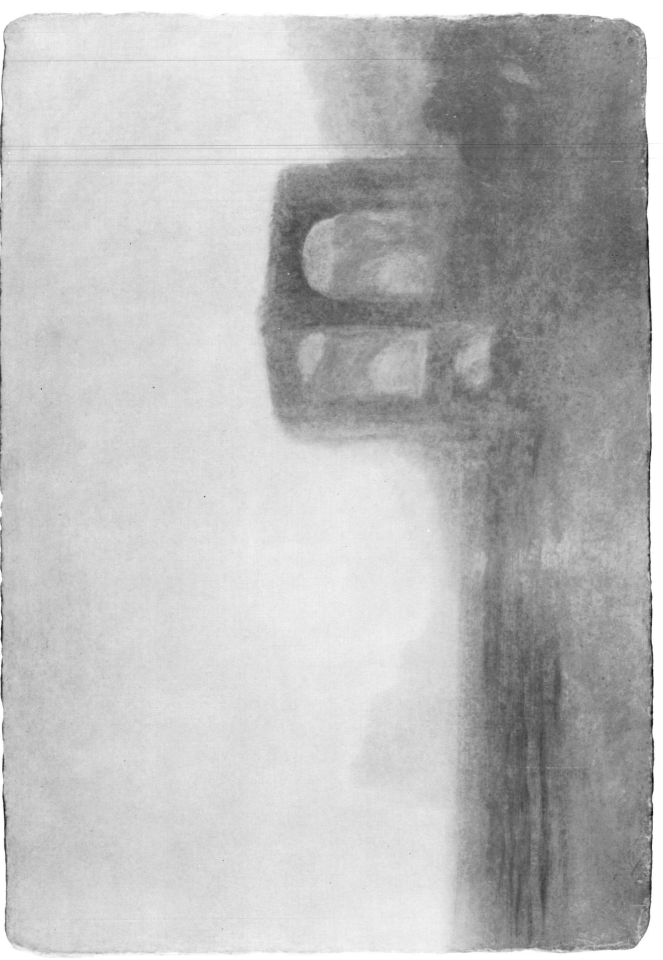

322. (Cat. 319) *Seacoast with Ruin, probably the Bay of Baiae*, 1828?; $16\frac{1}{4} \times 23\frac{11}{16}$; Tate Gallery

323. (Cat. 320) *Coast Scene near Naples*, 1828?; $16\frac{1}{8} \times 23\frac{1}{2}$; Tate Gallery

324. (Cat. 321)
Landscape with Trees and a Castle,
1828?;
$16\frac{5}{16} \times 23\frac{5}{8}$; Tate Gallery

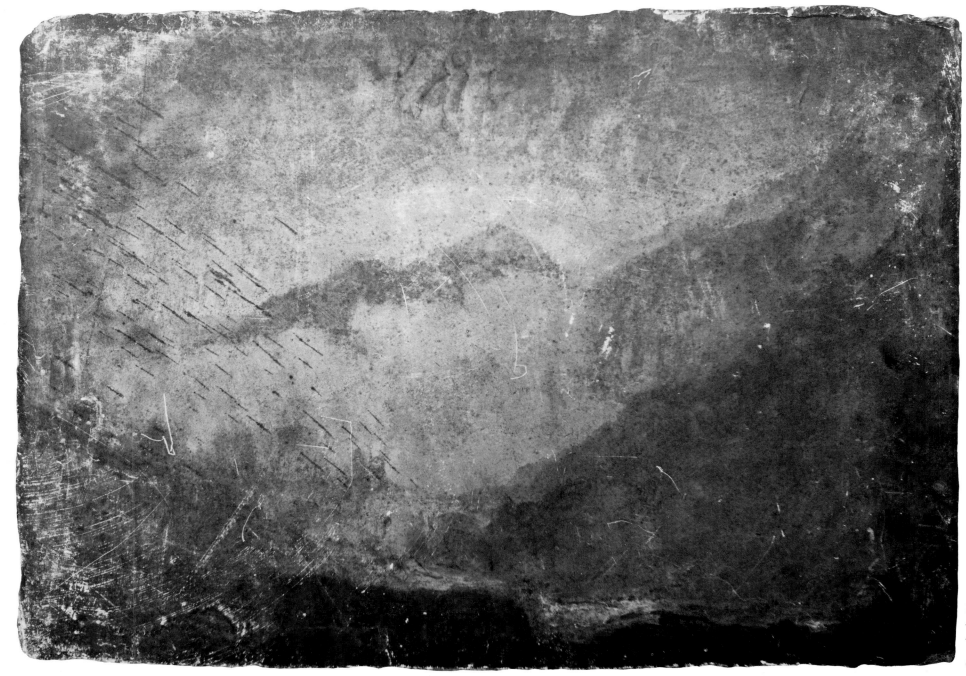

325. (Cat. 322) *Mountainous Landscape*, 1828?; $16\frac{1}{4} \times 23\frac{1}{2}$; Tate Gallery

326. (Cat. 323) *Hilly Landscape with Tower (?)* 1828?; $16\frac{9}{16} \times 20\frac{5}{8}$; Tate Gallery

327. (Cat. 324) *Landscape with a Tree on the Right*, 1828?; 11 × 16$\frac{3}{8}$; Tate Gallery

328. (Cat. 325) *Seascape with Burning Hulk*, 1828?; $9\frac{1}{2} \times 16\frac{3}{8}$; Tate Gallery

329. (Cat. 326) *A Seashore*, 1828?; $16\frac{3}{8} \times 20\frac{1}{2}$; Tate Gallery

330. (Cat. 327) *Seascape*, 1828?; $16\frac{1}{2} \times 20\frac{1}{2}$; Tate Gallery

331. (Cat. 330) *Ulysses deriding Polyphemus*, exh. 1829; $52\frac{1}{4} \times 80$; reproduced by courtesy of the Trustees, The National Gallery, London

332. (Cat. 328a) *A View on the Rhone (?)*, *c.*1828–9; $27\frac{15}{16} \times 20\frac{7}{8}$; Worcester Art Museum, Worcester, Mass.

333. (Cat. 333) *Jessica*, exh. 1830; 48 × 36; Petworth House

334. (Cat. 331) *The Loretto Necklace*, exh. 1829; $51\frac{1}{2} \times 68\frac{7}{8}$; Tate Gallery

335. (Cat. 332) *Pilate Washing his Hands*, exh. 1830; 36 × 48; Tate Gallery

336. (Cat. 334) *Calais Sands, Low Water, Poissards collecting Bait*, exh. 1830; $28\frac{1}{2} \times 42$; Bury Art Gallery

337. (Cat. 335) *Fish-Market on the Sands – the Sun rising through a Vapour*, exh. 1830; 34 × 44; destroyed

338. (Cat. 336) *Life-Boat and Manby Apparatus going off to a Stranded Vessel making Signal (Blue Lights) of Distress*, exh. 1831; 36 × 48; by courtesy of the Victoria and Albert Museum

339. (Cat. 337) *Caligula's Palace and Bridge*, exh. 1831; 54 × 97; Tate Gallery

340. (Cat. 338) *Lucy, Countess of Carlisle, and Dorothy Percy's Visit to their Father Lord Percy, when under Attainder*, exh. 1831; $15\frac{3}{4} \times 27\frac{1}{4}$; Tate Gallery

341. (Cat. 340) *Watteau Study by Fresnoy's Rules*, exh. 1831; $15\frac{3}{4} \times 27\frac{1}{4}$; Tate Gallery

342. (Cat. 339)
Admiral Van Tromp's Barge at the Entrance of the Texel, 1645,
exh. 1831; $35\frac{1}{2} \times 48$;
Trustees of Sir John Soane's Museum, London

343. (Cat. 341) *Fort Vimieux*, exh. 1831; 28 × 42; Private Collection, England

344. (Cat. 342) *Childe Harold's Pilgrimage – Italy*, exh. 1832; 56 × 97$\frac{3}{4}$; Tate Gallery

345. (Cat. 343) *The Prince of Orange, William III, embarked from Holland, and landed at Torbay, November 4th, 1688*, exh. 1832; $35\frac{1}{2} \times 47\frac{1}{4}$; Tate Gallery

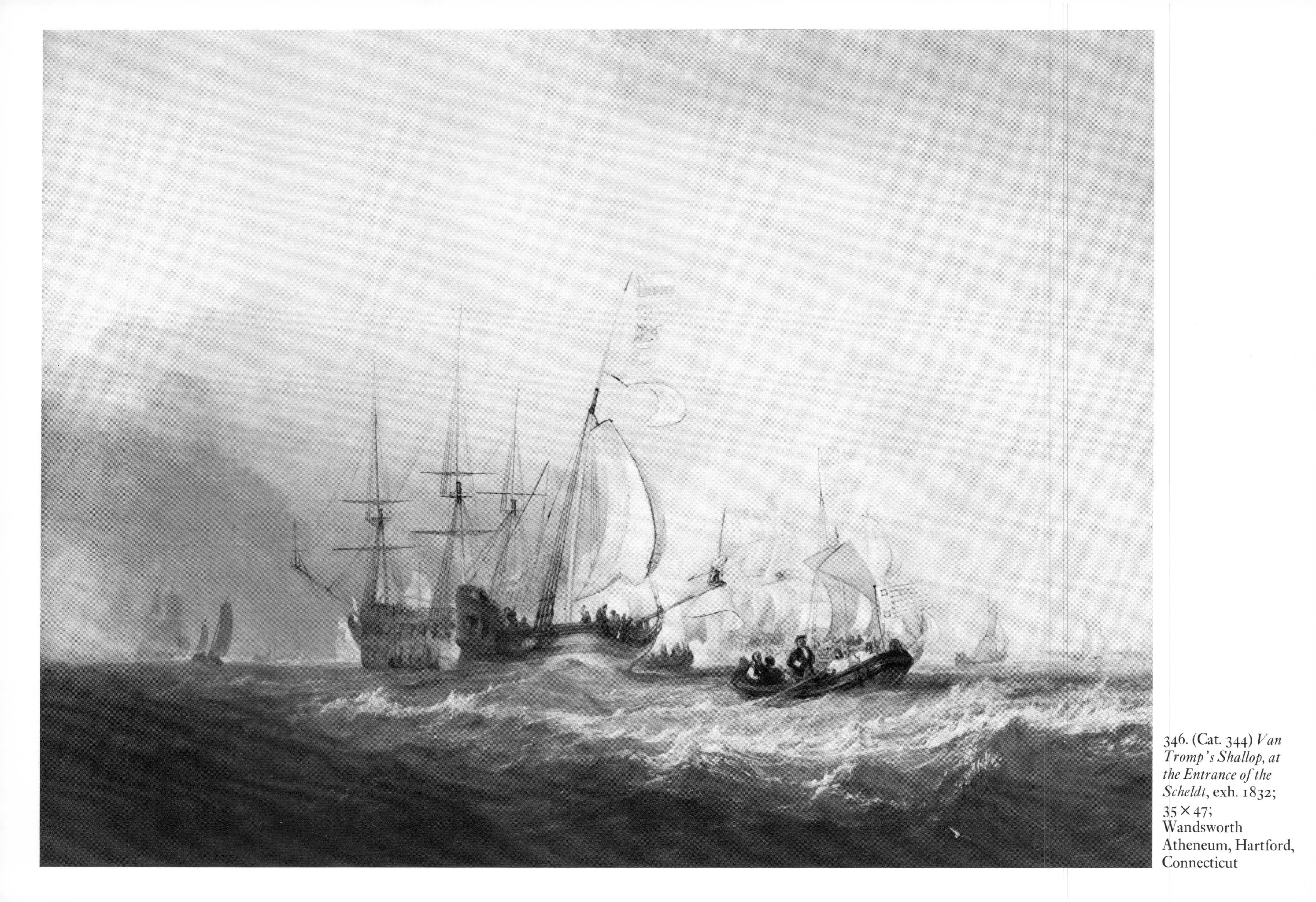

346. (Cat. 344) *Van Tromp's Shallop, at the Entrance of the Scheldt*, exh. 1832; 35 × 47; Wandsworth Atheneum, Hartford, Connecticut

347. (Cat. 345)
Helvoetsluys; – the City of Utrecht, 64, going to Sea, exh. 1832; 36 × 48; Private Collection, London

348. (Cat. 346) *Shadrach, Meshech and Abednego in the Burning Fiery Furnace*, exh. 1832; $36\frac{1}{16} \times 27\frac{7}{8}$; Tate Gallery

349. (Cat. 436) *Christ driving the Traders from the Temple*, *c.*1832; $36\frac{1}{4} \times 27\frac{3}{4}$; Tate Gallery

350. (Cat. 347) *Staffa, Fingal's Cave*, exh. 1832; 36 × 48; Yale Center for British Art, Paul Mellon Collection

351. (Cat. 348) *Rotterdam Ferry Boat*, exh. 1833; $36\frac{1}{2} \times 48\frac{1}{2}$; National Gallery of Art, Washington, D.C.

352. (Cat. 526) *A Mountain Lake at Sunset*, *c.*1830–35; $9\frac{1}{4} \times 6\frac{1}{8}$; Mr William Wood Prince, Chicago

353. (Cat. 352) After *Ducal Palace, Venice*, exh. 1833; engraving by W. Miller, 1854

354. (Cat. 350) *Van Goyen, looking out for a Subject*, exh. 1833; $36\frac{1}{2} \times 48\frac{3}{8}$; Copyright the Frick Collection, New York

355. (Cat. 351) *Van Tromp returning after the Battle of the Dogger Bank*, exh. 1833; $35\frac{5}{8} \times 47\frac{1}{2}$; Tate Gallery

356. (Cat. 349) *Bridge of Sighs, Ducal Palace and Custom-House, Venice: Canaletti painting*, exh. 1833; $20\frac{3}{16} \times 32\frac{7}{16}$; Tate Gallery

357. (Cat. 353) *Mouth of the Seine, Quille-Boeuf*, exh. 1833; $36 \times 48\frac{1}{2}$; Fundaçao Calouste Gulbenkian, Lisbon

358. (Cat. 354) *The Fountain of Indolence*, exh. 1834; $42 \times 65\frac{1}{2}$; the Beaverbrook Foundation

359. (Cat. 355) *The Golden Bough*, exh. 1834; 41 × 64½; Tate Gallery

360. (Cat. 357)
Wreckers – Coast of Northumberland, exh. 1834; 36 × 48; Yale Center for British Art, Paul Mellon Collection

361. (Cat. 358) *St Michael's Mount, Cornwall*, exh. 1834; $24 \times 30\frac{1}{2}$; by courtesy of the Victoria and Albert Museum

362. (Cat. 356)
Venice, exh. 1834;
$35\frac{1}{2} \times 48$; National
Gallery of Art,
Washington, D.C.

363. (Cat. 360)
Keelmen heaving in Coals by Night, exh. 1835; $35\frac{1}{2} \times 48$; National Gallery of Art, Washington, D.C.

364. (Cat. 359) *The Burning of the Houses of Lords and Commons, 16th October, 1834*, exh. 1835; $36\frac{1}{4} \times 48\frac{1}{2}$; Philadelphia Museum of Art

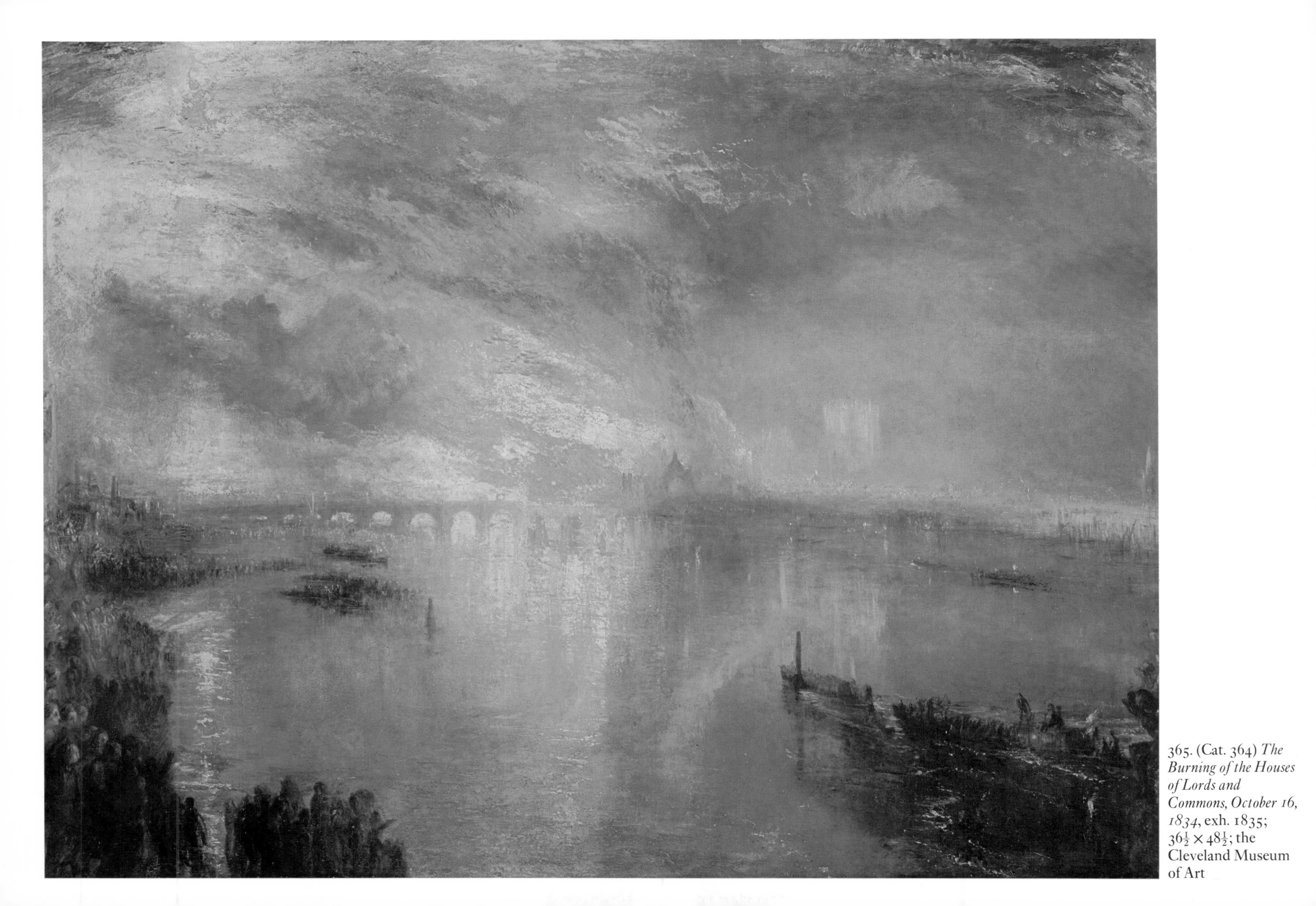

365. (Cat. 364) *The Burning of the Houses of Lords and Commons, October 16, 1834*, exh. 1835; $36\frac{1}{2} \times 48\frac{1}{2}$; the Cleveland Museum of Art

366. (Cat. 361) *The Bright Stone of Honour (Ehrenbreitstein)*, exh. 1835; $36\frac{1}{4} \times 48\frac{1}{2}$; Private Collection, London

367. (Cat. 362) *Venice, from the Porch of Madonna della Salute*, exh. 1835; 36 × 48; The Metropolitan Museum of Art, New York

368. (Cat. 363) *Line-Fishing, off Hastings*, exh. 1835; 23 × 30; by courtesy of the Victoria and Albert Museum

369. (Cat. 365) *Juliet and her Nurse*, exh. 1836; $36\frac{1}{2} \times 48\frac{1}{2}$; Sra. Amalia Lacroze de Fortabat, Argentina

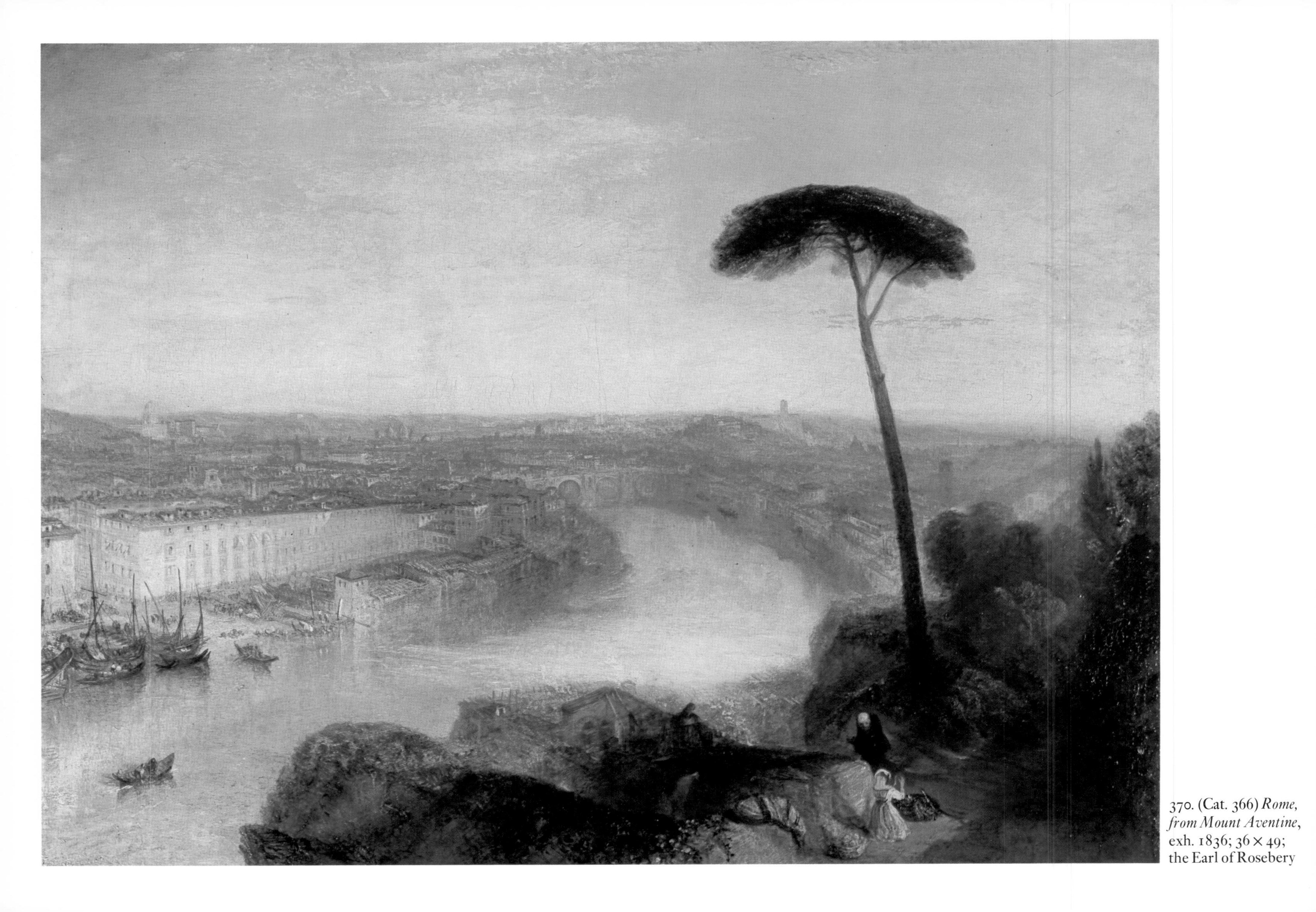

370. (Cat. 366) *Rome, from Mount Aventine*, exh. 1836; 36 × 49; the Earl of Rosebery

371. (Cat. 369) *Story of Apollo and Daphne*, exh. 1837; $43\frac{1}{4} \times 78\frac{1}{4}$; Tate Gallery

372. (Cat. 367) *Mercury and Argus*, exh. 1836; 59 × 43; National Gallery of Canada, Ottawa

373. (Cat. 368) *The Grand Canal, Venice*, exh. 1837; $58\frac{1}{4} \times 43\frac{1}{2}$; Henry E. Huntington Library and Art Gallery, San Marino, California

374. (Cat. 370) *The Parting of Hero and Leander*, exh. 1837; $57\frac{1}{2} \times 93$; reproduced by courtesy of the Trustees, The National Gallery, London

375. (Cat. 371) *Snow-Storm, Avalanche and Inundation – a Scene in the Upper Part of Val d'Aouste, Piedmont*, exh. 1837; $36\frac{1}{4} \times 48$; courtesy of the Art Institute of Chicago

376. (Cat. 374)
Modern Italy – the Pifferari, exh. 1838; $36\frac{1}{2} \times 48\frac{1}{2}$; Glasgow Art Gallery

377. (Cat. 375)
Ancient Italy – Ovid banished from Rome,
exh. 1838; $37\frac{1}{4} \times 49\frac{1}{4}$;
Private Collection

378. (Cat. 373) *Phryne going to the Public Baths as Venus*, exh. 1838; 76 × 65; Tate Gallery

379. (Cat. 382) *Bacchus and Ariadne*, exh. 1840; 31 × 31; Tate Gallery

380. (Cat. 372)
Fishing Boats with Hucksters bargaining for Fish, exh. 1838; $68\frac{5}{8} \times 88\frac{1}{4}$; courtesy of the Art Institute of Chicago

381. (Cat. 377) *The Fighting 'Temeraire', tugged to her Last Berth to be broken up, 1838*, exh. 1839; $35\frac{1}{4} \times 48$; reproduced by courtesy of the Trustees, The National Gallery, London

382. (Cat. 378) *Ancient Rome; Agrippina landing with the Ashes of Germanicus*, exh. 1839; 36 × 48; Tate Gallery

383. (Cat. 379) *Modern Rome – Campo Vaccino*, exh. 1839; $35\frac{1}{2} \times 48$; the Earl of Rosebery

384. (Cat. 380) *Pluto carrying off Proserpine*, exh. 1839; $36\frac{3}{8} \times 48\frac{5}{8}$; National Gallery of Art, Washington, D.C.

385. (Cat. 381) *Cicero at his Villa*, exh. 1839; $36\frac{1}{2} \times 48\frac{1}{2}$; Evelyn de Rothschild Esq., Ascott, Bucks

386. (Cat. 383) *Venice, the Bridge of Sighs*, exh. 1840; 24 × 36; Tate Gallery

387. (Cat. 384) *Venice, from the Canale della Giudecca, Chiesa di S. Maria della Salute*, exh. 1840; 24 × 36; by courtesy of the Victoria and Albert Museum

388. (Cat. 385) *Slavers throwing overboard the Dead and Dying*, exh. 1840; $35\frac{3}{4} \times 48$; Museum of Fine Arts, Boston

389. (Cat. 386) *The New Moon; or 'I've lost my Boat, You shan't have your Hoop'*, exh. 1840; $25\frac{3}{4} \times 32$; Tate Gallery

390. (Cat. 388) *Neapolitan Fisher-Girls surprised bathing by Moonlight*, exh. 1840?; $25\frac{5}{8} \times 31\frac{5}{8}$; Henry E. Huntington Library and Art Gallery, San Marino, California

391. (Cat. 389) *Neapolitan Fisher-Girls surprised bathing by Moonlight*, exh. 1840?; 25 × 31; Private Collection, U.S.A.

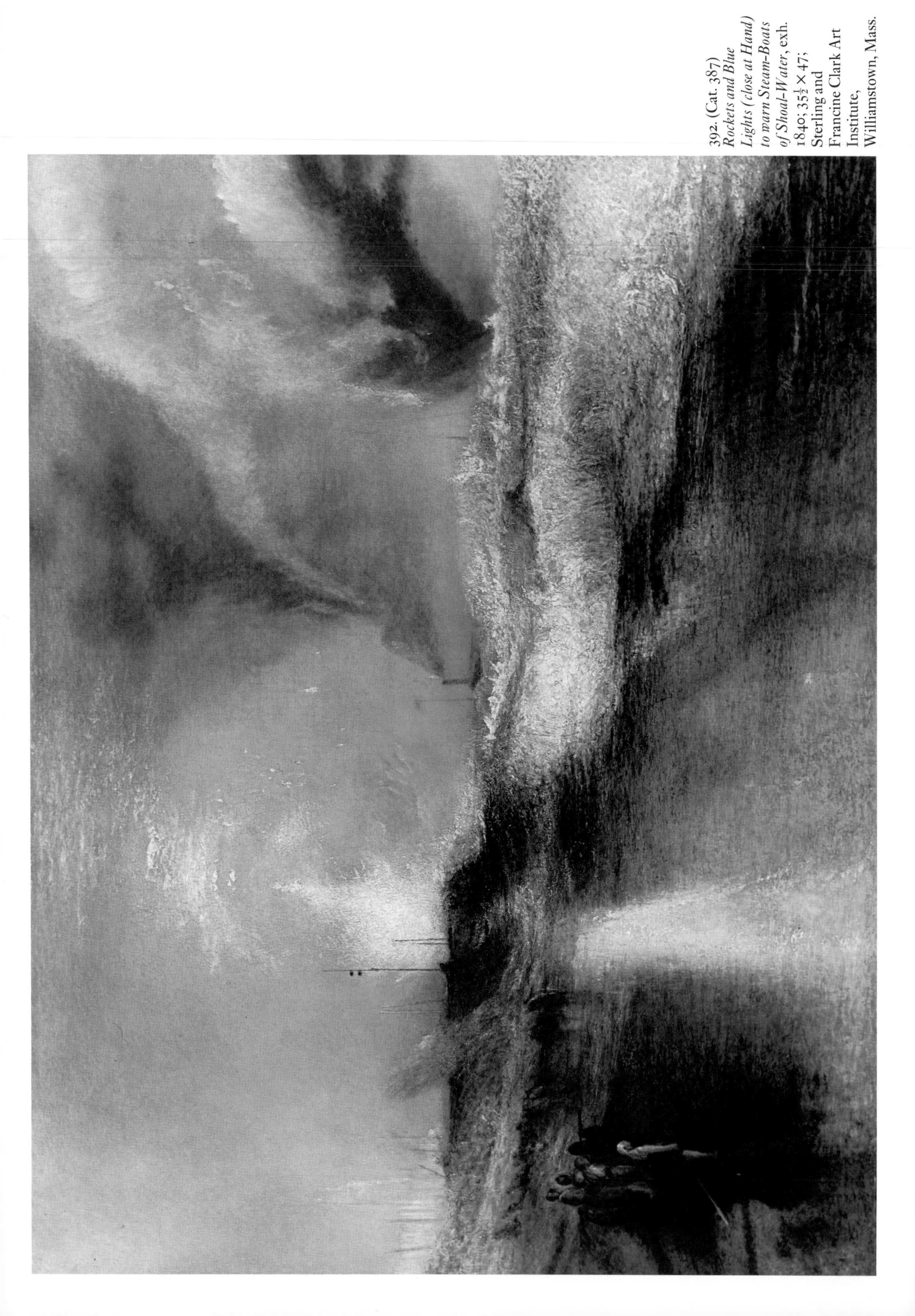

392. (Cat. 387)
Rockets and Blue Lights (close at Hand) to warn Steam-Boats of Shoal-Water, exh. 1840; $35\frac{1}{2} \times 47$; Sterling and Francine Clark Art Institute, Williamstown, Mass.

393. (Cat. 393) *Depositing of John Bellini's Three Pictures in la Chiesa Redentore, Venice*, exh. 1841; 29 × $45\frac{1}{2}$; Private Collection

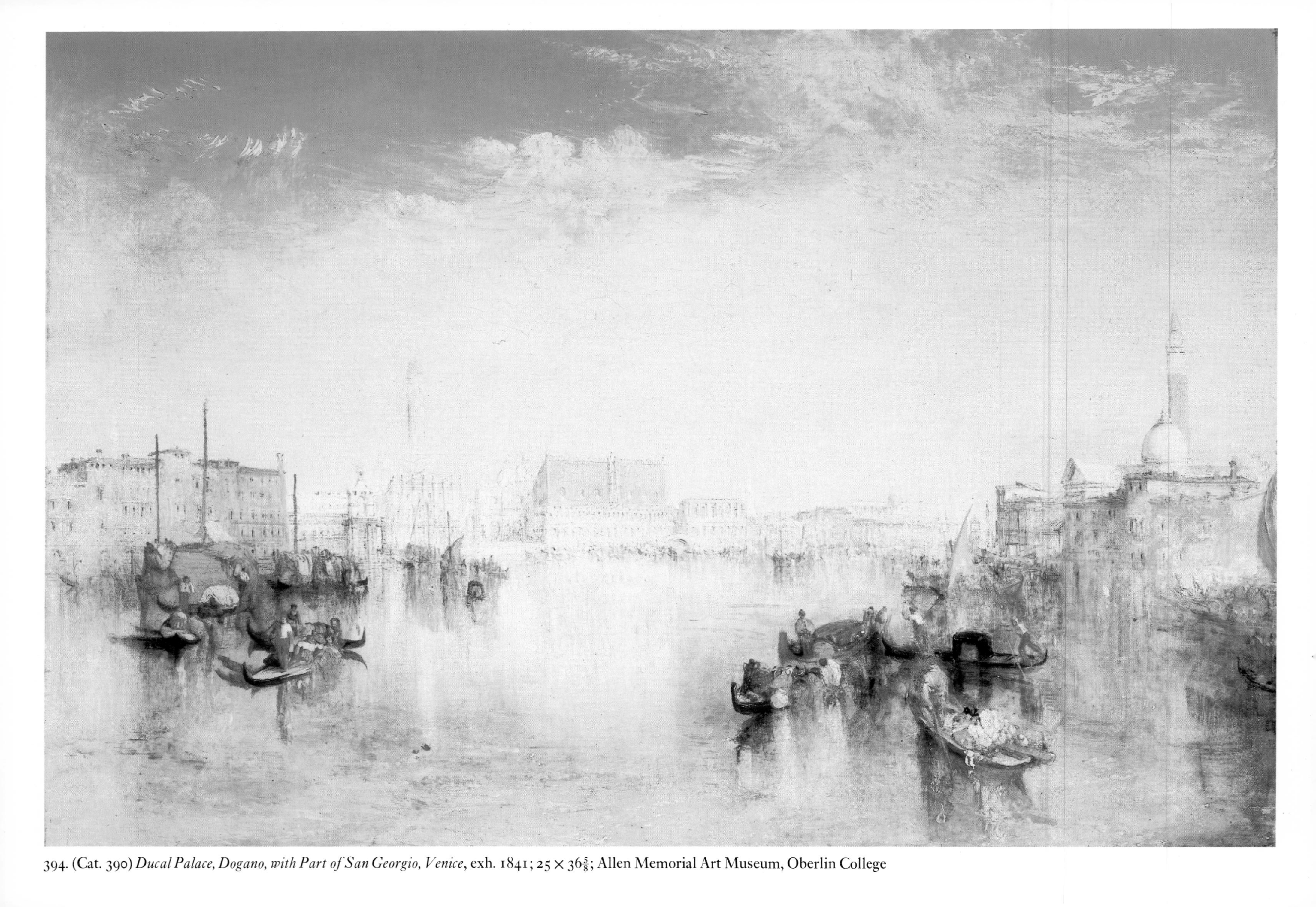

394. (Cat. 390) *Ducal Palace, Dogano, with Part of San Georgio, Venice*, exh. 1841; 25 × 36$\frac{5}{8}$; Allen Memorial Art Museum, Oberlin College

395. (Cat. 391) *Giudecca, la Donna della Salute and San Georgio*, exh. 1841; 24 × 36; Mr William Wood Prince and the Art Institute of Chicago

396. (Cat. 392) *Schloss Rosenau, Seat of H.R.H. Prince Albert of Coburg*, exh. 1841; $38\frac{1}{4} \times 49\frac{1}{8}$; Walker Art Gallery, Liverpool

397. (Cat. 442)
Rosenau, *c.*1841–4;
38 × 49; Yale Center
for British Art, Paul
Mellon Collection

398. (Cat. 394) *Dawn of Christianity (Flight into Egypt)*, exh. 1841; 31 × 31; Ulster Museum, Belfast

399. (Cat. 395) *Glaucus and Scylla*, exh. 1841; 31 × 30½; Kimbell Art Museum, Fort Worth, Texas

400. (Cat. 396) *The Dogano, San Giorgio, Citella, from the Steps of the Europa*, exh. 1842; $24\frac{1}{4} \times 36\frac{1}{2}$; Tate Gallery

401. (Cat. 397) *Campo Santo, Venice*, exh. 1842; $24\frac{1}{2} \times 36\frac{1}{2}$; Toledo Museum of Art, Toledo, Ohio

402. (Cat. 399) *Peace – Burial at Sea*, exh. 1842; $34\frac{1}{4} \times 34\frac{1}{8}$; Tate Gallery

403. (Cat. 400) *War. The Exile and the Rock Limpet*, exh. 1842; $31\frac{1}{4} \times 31\frac{1}{4}$; Tate Gallery

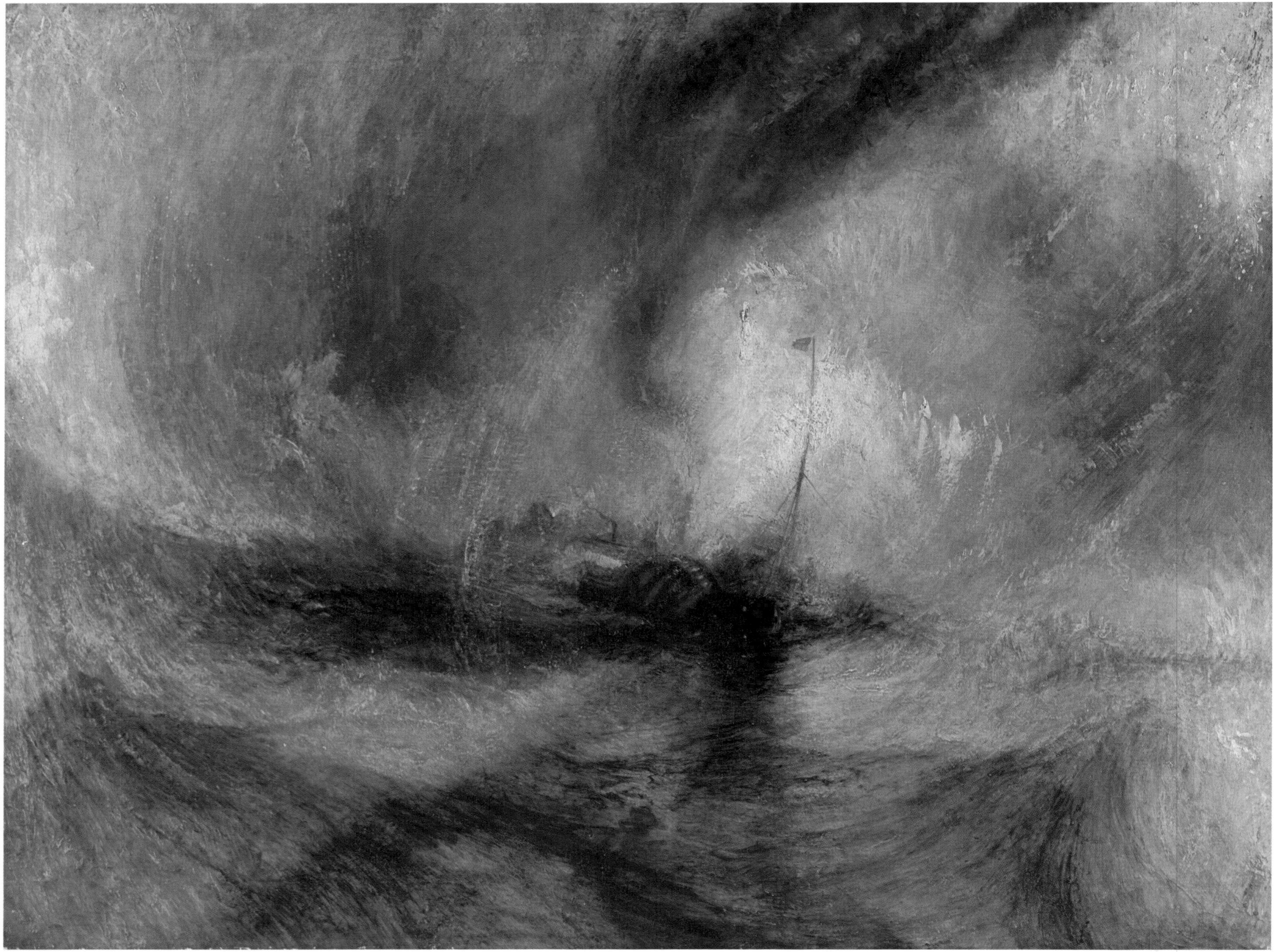

404. (Cat. 398) *Snow Storm – Steam-Boat off a Harbour's Mouth*, exh. 1842; 36 × 48; Tate Gallery

405. (Cat. 443) *The Evening of the Deluge*, *c.*1843; $29\frac{7}{8} \times 29\frac{7}{8}$; National Gallery of Art, Washington, D.C.

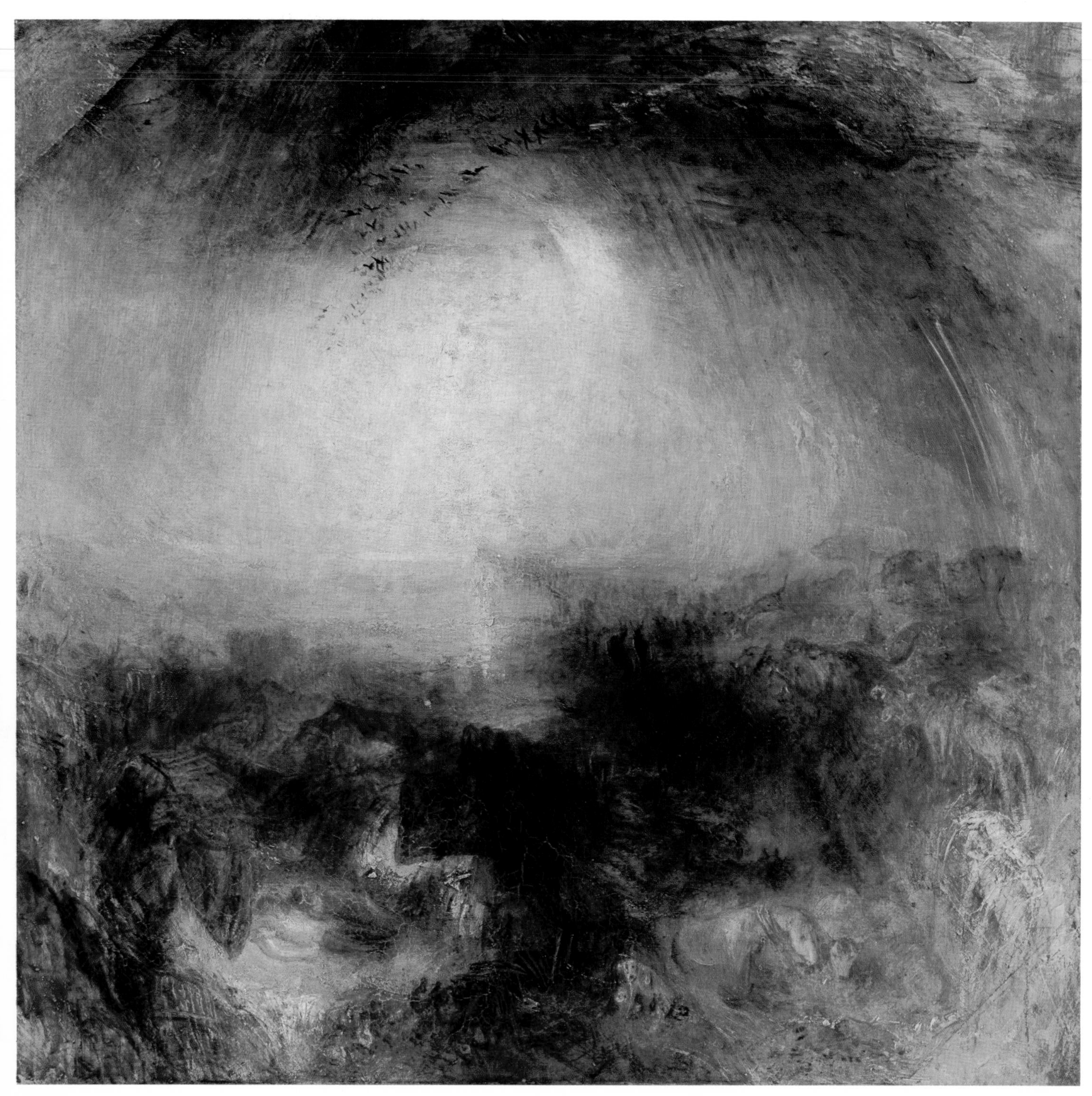

406. (Cat. 404) *Shade and Darkness – the Evening of the Deluge*, exh. 1843; 31 × 30¾; Tate Gallery

407. (Cat. 405) *Light and Colour (Goethe's Theory) – the Morning after the Deluge – Moses writing the Book of Genesis*, exh. 1843; 31 × 31; Tate Gallery

408. (Cat. 402) *The Sun of Venice going to Sea*, exh. 1843; $24\frac{1}{4} \times 36\frac{1}{4}$; Tate Gallery

409. (Cat. 403) *Dogana, and Madonna della Salute, Venice*, exh. 1843; $24\frac{3}{4} \times 36\frac{5}{8}$; National Gallery of Art, Washington, D.C.

410. (Cat. 401) *The Opening of the Walhalla, 1842*, exh. 1843; $44\frac{5}{16} \times 79$; Tate Gallery

411. (Cat. 406) *St Benedetto, looking towards Fusina*, exh. 1843; $24\frac{1}{2} \times 36\frac{1}{2}$; Tate Gallery

412. (Cat. 407)
Ostend, exh. 1844;
$36\frac{1}{2} \times 48\frac{1}{2}$; Neue
Pinakothek,
Munich

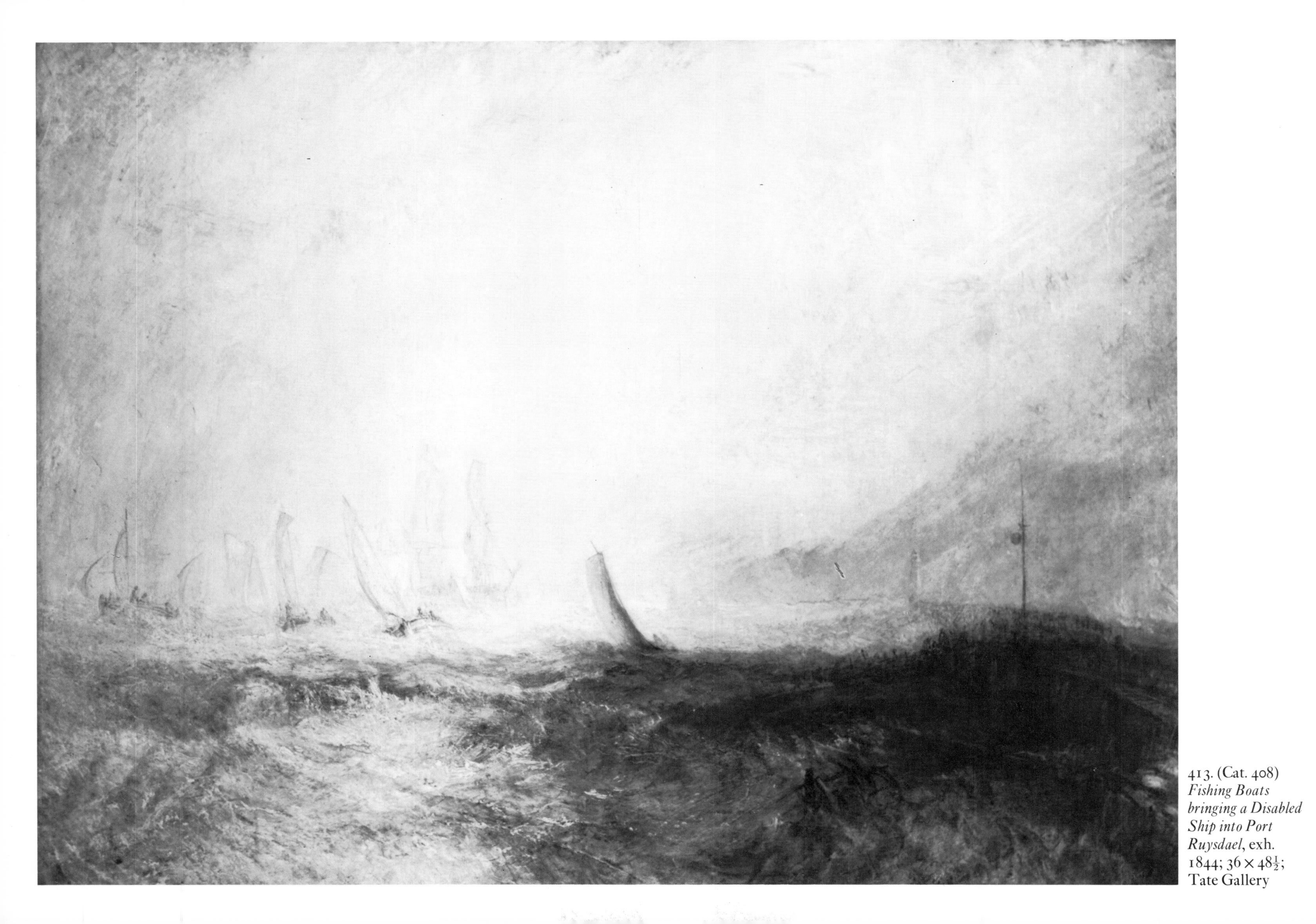

413. (Cat. 408) *Fishing Boats bringing a Disabled Ship into Port Ruysdael*, exh. 1844; 36 × 48½; Tate Gallery

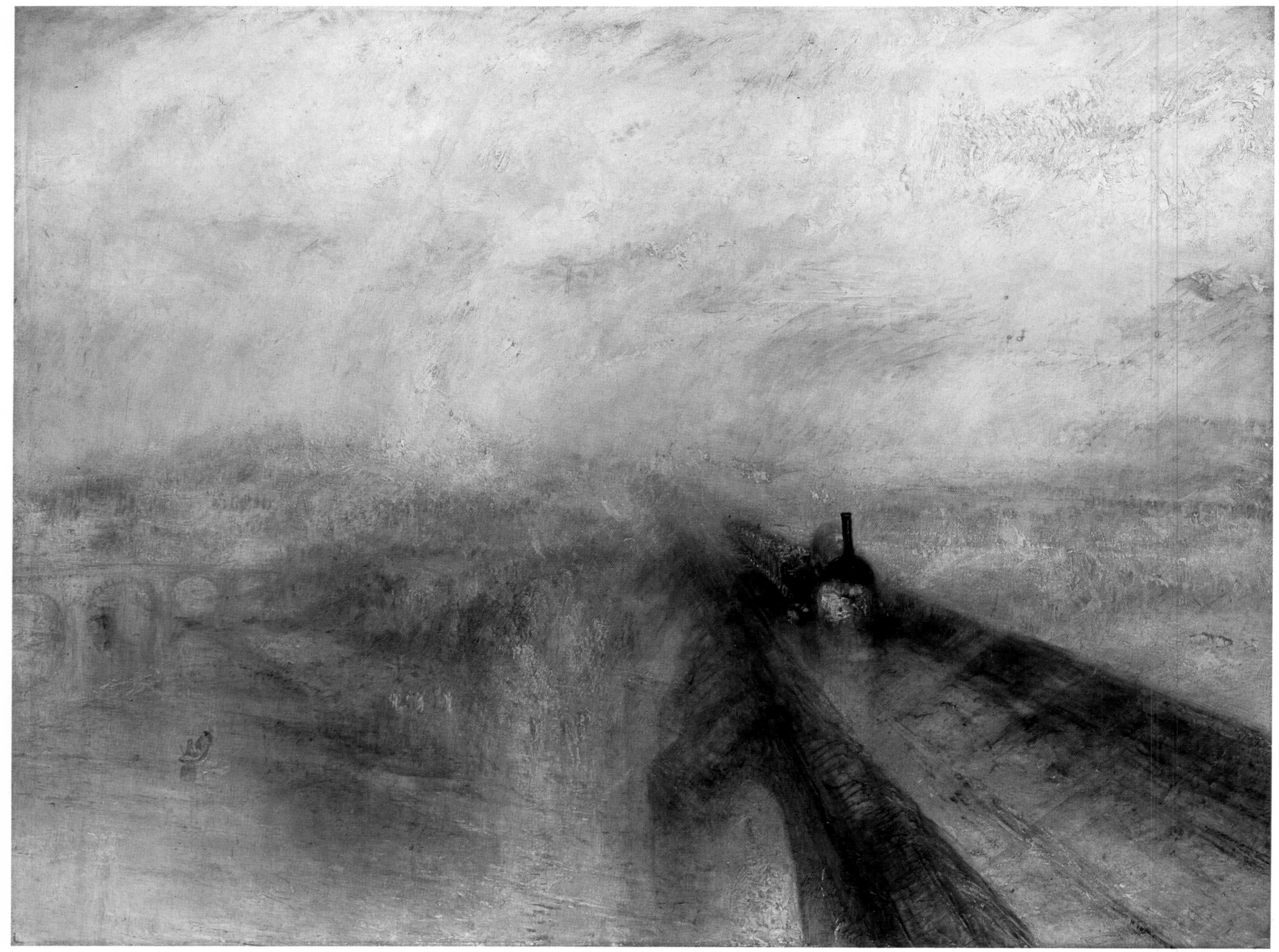

414. (Cat. 409)
Rain, Steam, and Speed – the Great Western Railway, exh. 1844;
$35\frac{3}{4} \times 48$;
reproduced by courtesy of the Trustees, The National Gallery, London

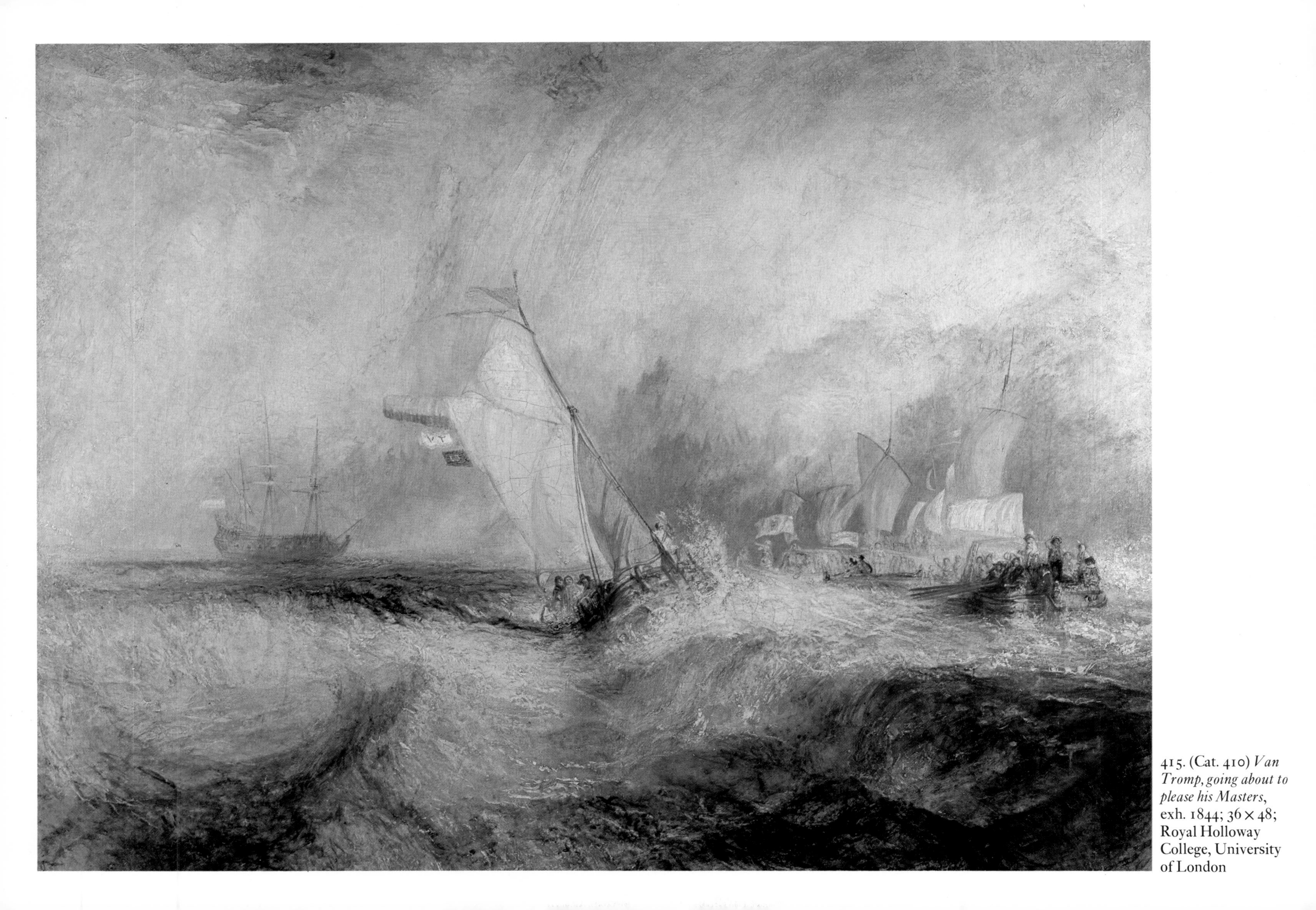

415. (Cat. 410) *Van Tromp, going about to please his Masters*, exh. 1844; 36 × 48; Royal Holloway College, University of London

416. (Cat. 411) *Venice – Maria della Salute*, exh. 1844; $24\frac{1}{8} \times 36\frac{1}{4}$; Tate Gallery

417. (Cat. 412) *Approach to Venice*, exh. 1844; $24\frac{1}{2} \times 37$; National Gallery of Art, Washington, D.C.

418. (Cat. 413) *Venice Quay, Ducal Palace*, exh. 1844; $24\frac{1}{2} \times 36\frac{1}{2}$; Tate Gallery

419. (Cat. 420) *Queen Mab's Cave*, exh. 1846; $36\frac{1}{4} \times 48\frac{1}{4}$; Tate Gallery

420. (Cat. 416) *Venice, Evening, going to the Ball*, exh. 1845; $24\frac{1}{4} \times 36\frac{3}{8}$; Tate Gallery

421. (Cat. 417) *Morning, returning from the Ball, St. Martino*, exh. 1845; $24\frac{1}{2} \times 36\frac{1}{2}$; Tate Gallery

422. (Cat. 418) *Venice – Noon*, exh. 1845; $24 \times 36\frac{1}{8}$; Tate Gallery

423. (Cat. 419) *Venice – Sunset, a Fisher*, exh. 1845; $24\frac{1}{8} \times 36\frac{1}{4}$; Tate Gallery

424. (Cat. 414)
Whalers, exh. 1845; $35\frac{7}{8} \times 48$; Tate Gallery

425. (Cat. 415)
Whalers, exh. 1845;
$36\frac{1}{8} \times 48\frac{1}{4}$; The
Metropolitan
Museum of Art, New
York

426. (Cat. 423)
'Hurrah! for the Whaler Erebus! another Fish!', exh. 1846; $35\frac{1}{2} \times 47\frac{1}{2}$; Tate Gallery

427. (Cat. 426) *Whalers (boiling Blubber) entangled in Flaw Ice*, exh. 1846; $35\frac{3}{8} \times 47\frac{1}{4}$; Tate Gallery

428. (Cat. 421) *Going to the Ball (San Martino)*, exh. 1846; 24 × 36; Oakpict Inc.

429. (Cat. 422) *Returning from the Ball (St Martha)*, exh. 1846; 24 × 36; Oakpict Inc.

430. (Cat. 424) *Undine giving the Ring to Massaniello, Fisherman of Naples*, exh. 1846; 31⅛ × 31⅛; Tate Gallery

431. (Cat. 425) *The Angel standing in the Sun*, exh. 1846; 31 × 31; Tate Gallery

432. (Cat. 427) *The Hero of a Hundred Fights*, *c.*1800–10, (reworked and exh. 1847); $35\frac{3}{4} \times 47\frac{3}{4}$; Tate Gallery

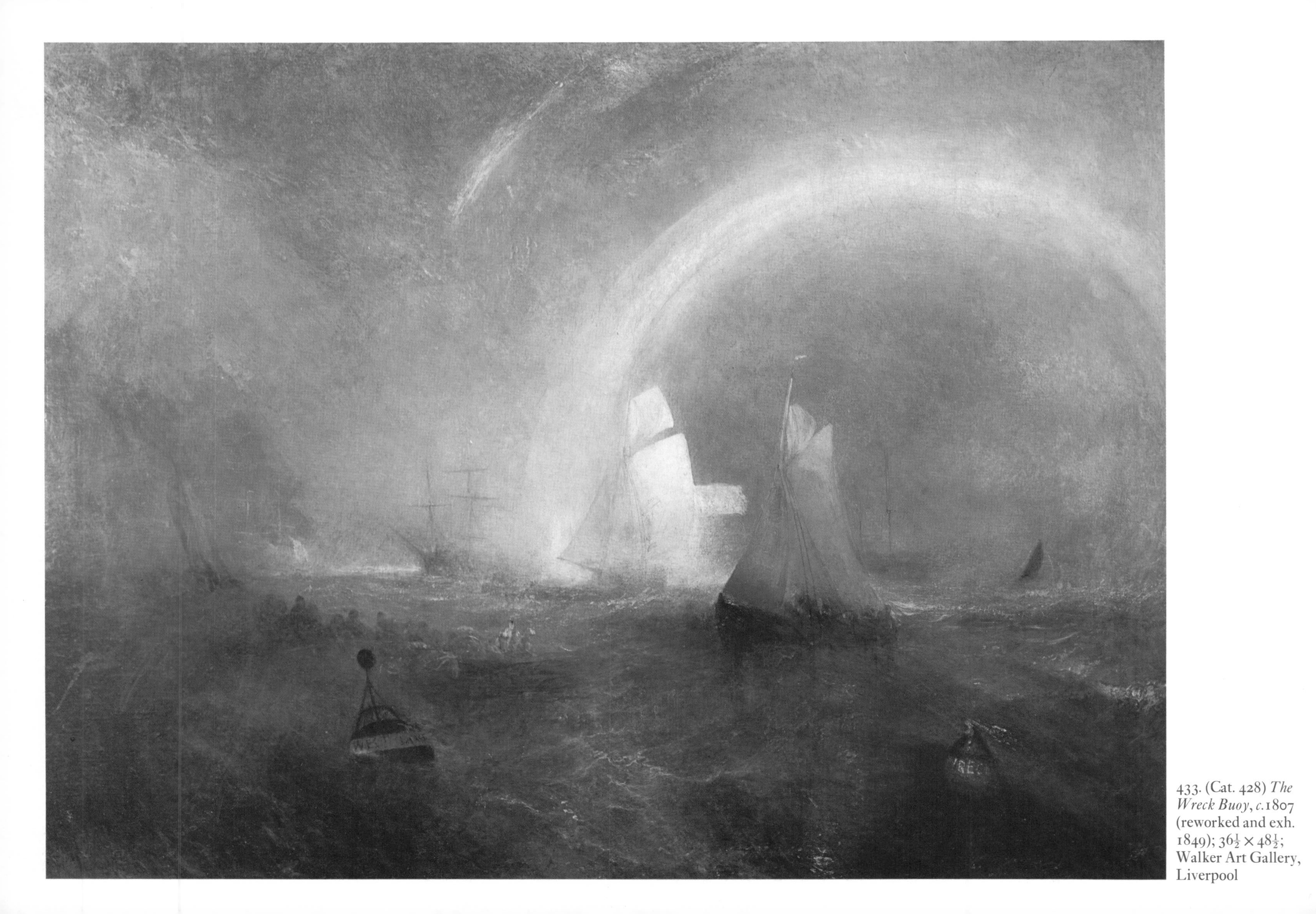

433. (Cat. 428) *The Wreck Buoy*, *c.*1807 (reworked and exh. 1849); $36\frac{1}{2} \times 48\frac{1}{2}$; Walker Art Gallery, Liverpool

434. (Cat. 429)
Mercury sent to admonish Æneas,
exh. 1850;
$35\frac{1}{2} \times 47\frac{1}{2}$; Tate Gallery

435. (Cat. 430) *Æneas relating his Story to Dido*, exh. 1850; 36 × 48; destroyed?, formerly Tate Gallery (from 1906 reproduction)

436. (Cat. 431) *The Visit to the Tomb*, exh. 1850; 36 × 48; Tate Gallery

437. (Cat. 432) *The Departure of the Fleet*, exh. 1850; $35\frac{3}{8} \times 47\frac{3}{8}$; Tate Gallery

438. (Cat. 433) *Landscape: Christ and the Woman of Samaria*, *c.*1830; $57\frac{1}{4} \times 93\frac{1}{2}$; Tate Gallery

439. (Cat. 434) *Rocky Bay with Figures*, *c.*1830; 36 × 49; Tate Gallery

440. (Cat. 437) *Tivoli: Tobias and the Angel*, *c.*1835; $35\frac{5}{8} \times 47\frac{5}{8}$; Tate Gallery

441. (Cat. 438) *The Arch of Constantine, Rome*, *c.*1835; 36 × 48; Tate Gallery

442. (Cat. 435) *The Vision of Jacob's Ladder*, *c.*1830?; $48\frac{1}{2} \times 74$; Tate Gallery

443. (Cat. 440) *Heidelberg*, *c.*1840–45; 52 × 79½; Tate Gallery

444. (Cat. 439) *Mountain Glen, perhaps with Diana and Actaeon*, *c.*1835–40; $58\frac{3}{4} \times 43\frac{3}{4}$; Tate Gallery

445. (Cat. 444) *A Lady in Van Dyck Costume*, *c.*1830–35; $47\frac{3}{4} \times 35\frac{7}{8}$; Tate Gallery

446. (Cat. 445) *Dinner in a Great Room*, *c.*1830–35; $35\frac{3}{4} \times 48$; Tate Gallery

447. (Cat. 446) *Figures in a Building*, *c.*1830–35; 36 × 48; Tate Gallery

448. (Cat. 447) *Music at East Cowes Castle*, *c.*1835; $47\frac{3}{4} \times 35\frac{5}{8}$; Tate Gallery

449. (Cat. 448) *Two Women and a Letter*, *c.*1835; 48 × 36; Tate Gallery

450. (Cat. 449)
Interior at Petworth, *c.*1837; $35\frac{3}{4} \times 48$; Tate Gallery

451. (Cat. 450) *A Vaulted Hall*, *c.*1835; $29\frac{1}{2} \times 36$; Tate Gallery

452. (Cat. 451) *The Cave of Despair (?)*, *c.*1835; 20 × 32; Tate Gallery

453. (Cat. 452) *Head of a Person asleep*, *c.*1835; $9\frac{5}{8} \times 11\frac{7}{8}$; Tate Gallery

454. (Cat. 453)
The Evening Star, *c.*1830; $36\frac{1}{4} \times 48\frac{1}{4}$; reproduced by courtesy of the Trustees, The National Gallery, London

455. (Cat. 454) *Hastings*, *c.*1830–35; 35½ × 48; Tate Gallery

456. (Cat. 455) *Rough Sea with Wreckage*, *c*.1830–35; $36\frac{1}{4} \times 48\frac{1}{4}$; Tate Gallery

457. (Cat. 456) *Breakers on a Flat Beach*, *c.*1830–35; $35\frac{1}{2} \times 47\frac{5}{8}$; Tate Gallery

458. (Cat. 457) *Waves breaking against the Wind*, *c.*1835; 23 × 35; Tate Gallery

459. (Cat. 458) *Waves breaking on a Lee Shore*, *c.*1835; $23\frac{1}{2} \times 37\frac{1}{2}$; Tate Gallery

460. (Cat. 459)
Waves breaking on a Shore, *c.*1835; $18\frac{1}{4} \times 23\frac{7}{8}$; Tate Gallery

461. (Cat. 460) *Fire at Sea*, *c.*1835; $67\frac{1}{2} \times 86\frac{3}{4}$; Tate Gallery

462. (Cat. 461) *Yacht approaching the Coast*, *c.*1835–40; $40\frac{1}{4} \times 56$; Tate Gallery

463. (Cat. 462)
Stormy Sea with Blazing Wreck,
*c.*1835–40;
$39\frac{1}{8} \times 55\frac{3}{4}$; Tate Gallery

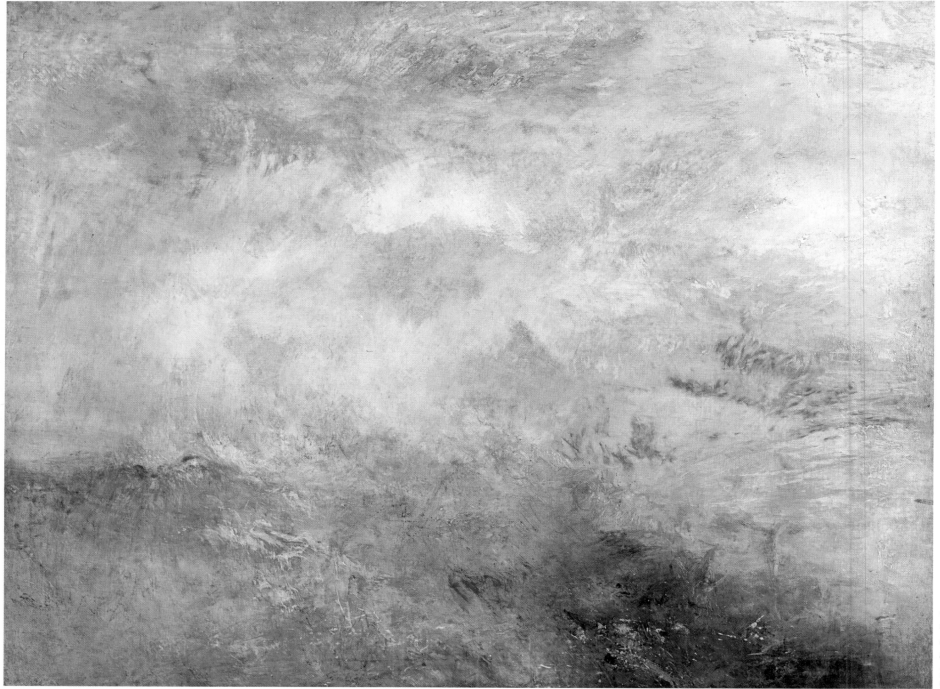

464. (Cat. 463) *Stormy Sea with Dolphins*, *c.*1835–40; 35¾ × 48; Tate Gallery

465. (Cat. 464)
Margate (?) from the Sea, *c.*1835–40;
$36\frac{1}{8} \times 48\frac{1}{4}$;
reproduced by courtesy of the Trustees, The National Gallery, London

466. (Cat. 465)
Seascape,
*c.*1835–40;
$35\frac{1}{2} \times 47\frac{5}{8}$; Tate Gallery

467. (Cat. 466) *Seascape with Storm coming on*, *c*.1840; 36 × 47$\frac{7}{8}$; Tate Gallery

468. (Cat. 467) *Seascape with Distant Coast*, *c.*1840; 36 × 48; Tate Gallery

469. (Cat. 468)
Seascape with Buoy,
*c.*1840; 36 × 48; Tate
Gallery

470. (Cat. 469) *Sun setting over a Lake*, *c.*1840; $35\frac{7}{8} \times 48\frac{1}{4}$; Tate Gallery

471. (Cat. 470) *A Wreck, with Fishing Boats*, *c.*1840–45; $36 \times 48\frac{1}{8}$; Tate Gallery

472. (Cat. 471) *Rough Sea*, *c*.1840–45; 36 × 48; Tate Gallery

473. (Cat. 472)
Seascape: Folkestone,
*c.*1845; $34\frac{3}{4} \times 46\frac{1}{4}$;
Private Collection

474. (Cat. 473)
Sunrise with Sea Monsters, *c.*1845;
36 × 48; Tate Gallery

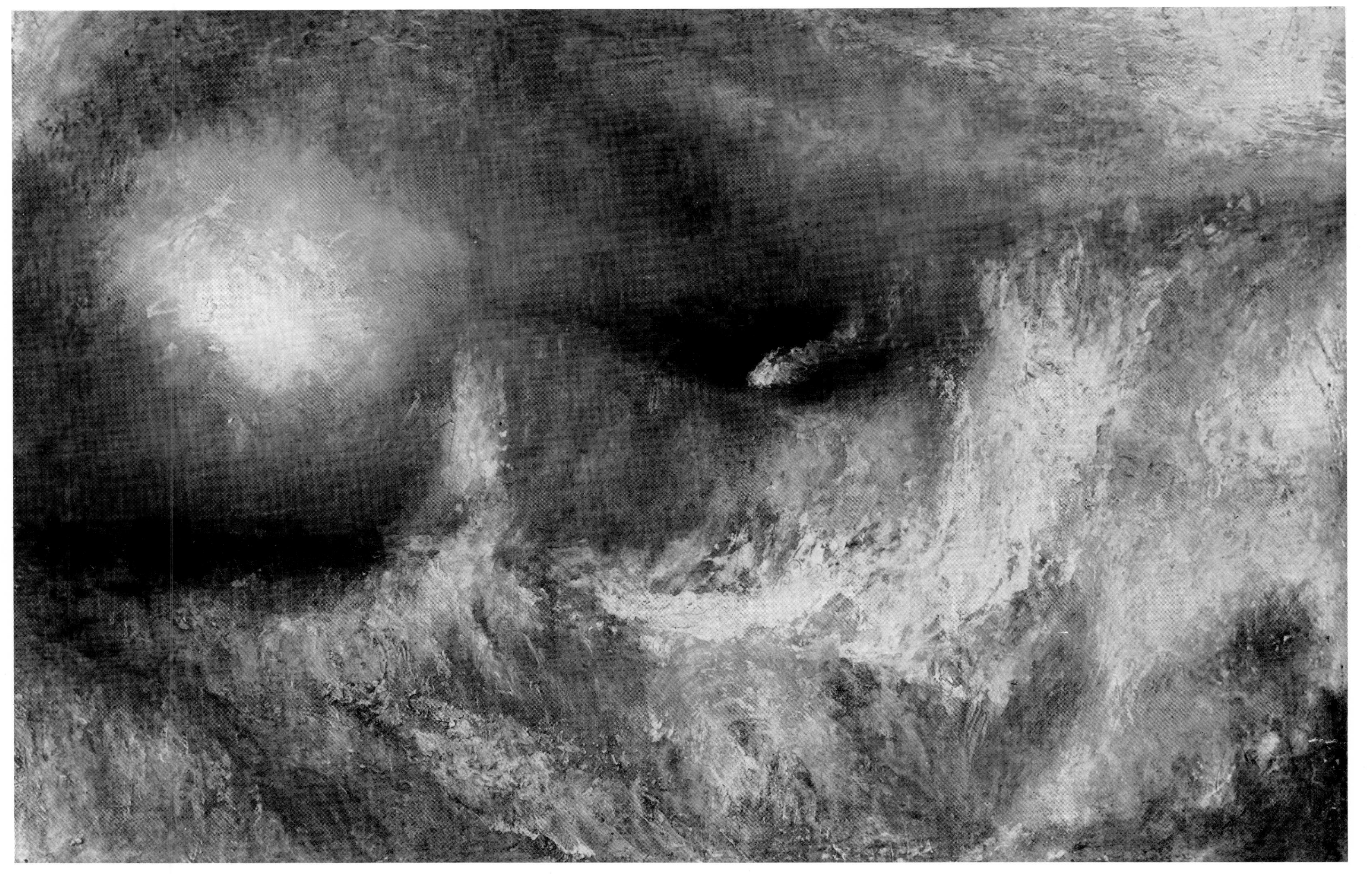

475. (Cat. 474) *The Beacon Light*, *c.*1835–40; $23\frac{1}{2} \times 36\frac{1}{2}$; National Museum of Wales

476. (Cat. 475)
Margate Harbour,
*c.*1835–40;
$18\frac{1}{16} \times 24\frac{1}{16}$;
Walker Art
Gallery,
Liverpool

477. (Cat. 476) *Off the Nore: Wind and Water*, *c.*1840–5; 12 × 18; Yale Center for British Art, Paul Mellon Collection

478. (Cat. 477) *Wreckers on the Coast: Sun rising through Mist*, *c.*1835–40; 14 × 21$\frac{3}{4}$; Private Collection, Germany

479. (Cat. 478) *Morning after the Wreck*, *c.*1835–40; 15 × 24; National Museum of Wales

480. (Cat. 479) *Off Ramsgate (?)*, *c.*1840; $12\frac{1}{4} \times 19$; Private Collection, U.S.A.

481. (Cat. 480) *The Storm*, *c.*1840–45; $12\frac{3}{4} \times 21\frac{1}{2}$; National Museum of Wales

482. (Cat. 481) *The Day after the Storm*, *c.*1840–45; 12 × 21; National Museum of Wales

483. (Cat. 482) *Waves breaking on the Shore*, *c.*1840–5; $17\frac{1}{2} \times 25$; Yale Center for British Art, Paul Mellon Collection

484. (Cat. 483) *Off Deal*, *c.*1835; $9 \times 11\frac{15}{16}$; Nationalmuseum, Stockholm

485. (Cat. 484) *A Sailing Boat off Deal*, *c.*1835; 9 × 12; National Museum of Wales

486. (Cat. 485)
Riders on a Beach,
c.1835; 9 × 12;
British Museum

487. (Cat. 486)
Shore Scene with Waves and Breakwater, c.1835; 9 × 12; British Museum

488. (Cat. 487) *Coast Scene with Buildings*, *c.*1840–45?; 12 × 18¾; British Museum

489. (Cat. 488) *Red Sky over a Beach*, *c.*1840–45?; 11$\frac{15}{16}$ × 18$\frac{7}{8}$; British Museum

490. (Cat. 489) *Ship in a Storm*, *c.*1840–45?; $11\frac{7}{8} \times 18\frac{3}{4}$; British Museum

491. (Cat. 490) *Calm Sea with Distant Grey Clouds*, *c.*1840–45?; 11⅞ × 19; British Museum

492. (Cat. 491) *Coast Scene with Breaking Waves*, *c.*1840–45?; $11\frac{5}{8} \times 19\frac{1}{8}$; British Museum

493. (Cat. 492) *Sea, Sand and Sky (?)*, *c.*1840–45?; $11\frac{3}{4} \times 18\frac{1}{8}$; British Museum

494. (Cat. 493) *Sand and Sky (?)*, *c.*1840–45?; 11 13/16 × 18 7/8; British Museum

495. (Cat. 494) *Yellow Sky?*, *c.*1840–45?; $11\frac{7}{8} \times 18\frac{3}{4}$; British Museum

496. (Cat. 495) *Coast Scene*, *c.*1840–45?; $10\frac{5}{8} \times 11\frac{15}{16}$; British Museum

497. (Cat. 496) *Figures on a Beach*, *c.*1840–45?; $10\frac{3}{16} \times 11\frac{3}{4}$; British Museum

498. (Cat. 497) *Sunset seen from a Beach with Breakwater*, *c.*1840–45?; $9\frac{3}{4} \times 11\frac{7}{8}$; British Museum

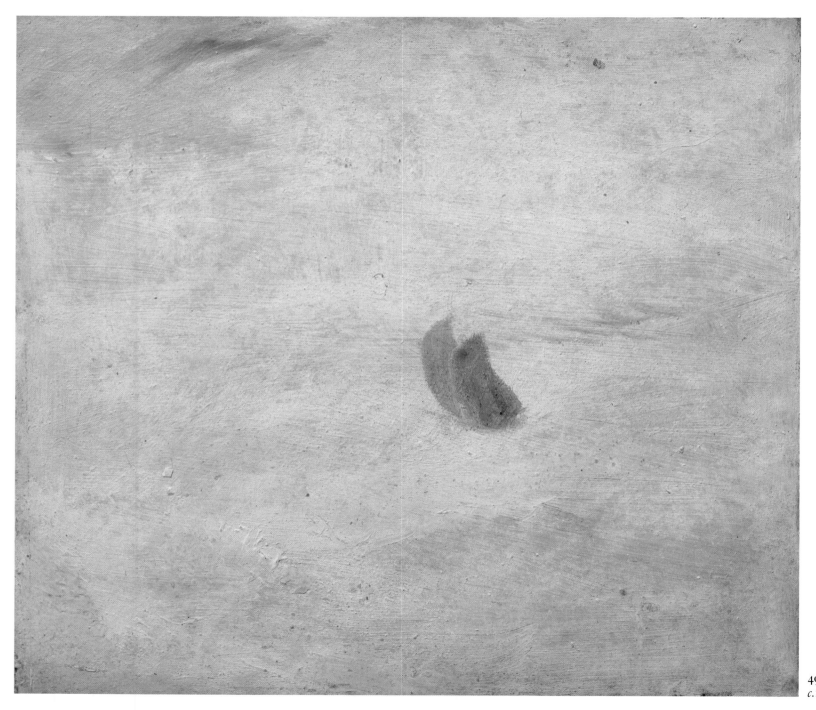

499. (Cat. 498) *Sailing Boat in a Rough Sea*, *c.*1840–45?; $10\frac{1}{2} \times 11\frac{15}{16}$; British Museum

500. (Cat. 499)
Two Figures on a Beach with a Boat, *c.*1840–45?; $9\frac{5}{8} \times 13\frac{5}{8}$; British Museum

501. (Cat. 500) *Waves breaking on a Beach*, *c.*1840–45?; $9\frac{3}{4} \times 13\frac{1}{2}$; British Museum

502. (Cat. 502) *Venice with the Salute*, *c.*1840–45; $24\frac{1}{2} \times 36\frac{1}{2}$; Tate Gallery

503. (Cat. 503) *Scene in Venice*, *c.*1840–45; $24\frac{1}{2} \times 36\frac{1}{2}$; Tate Gallery

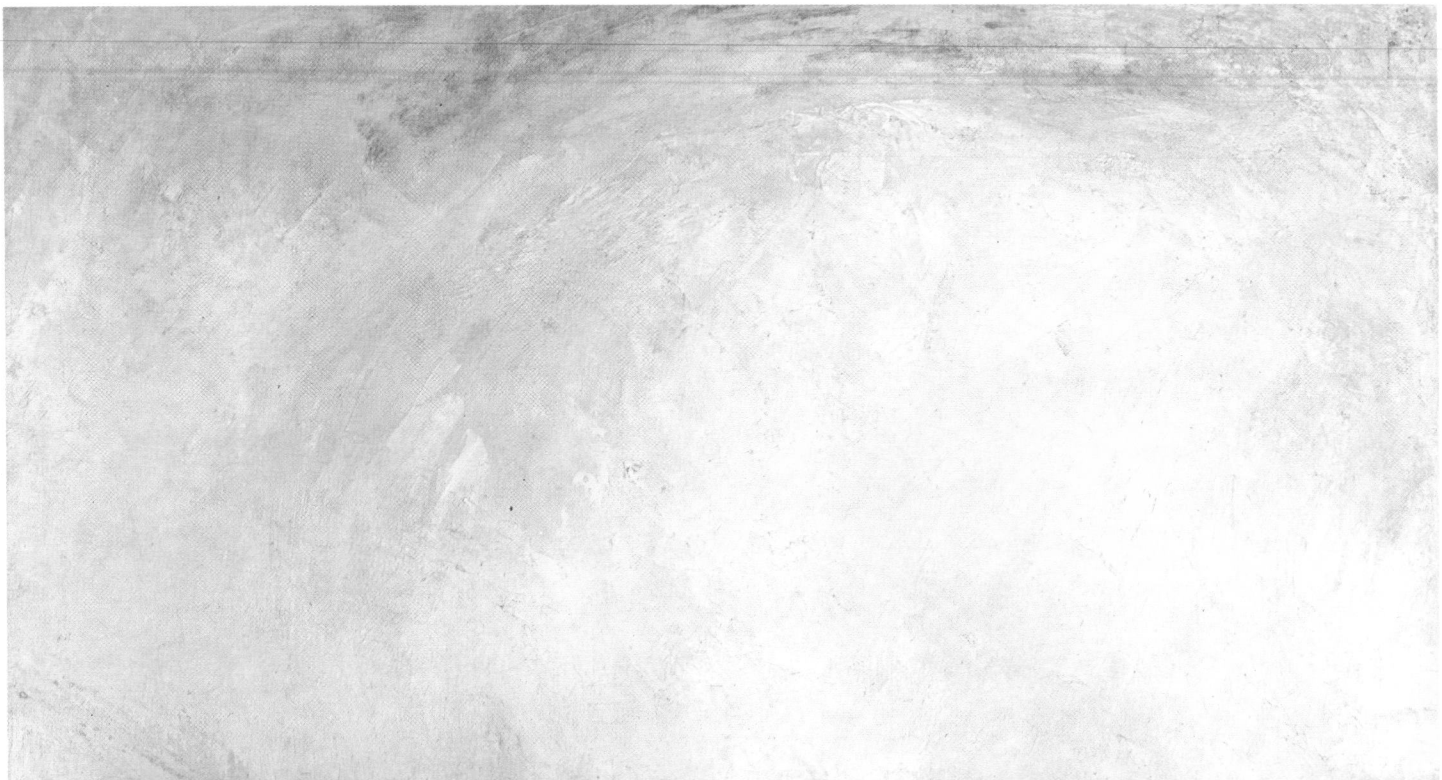

504. (Cat. 504) *Venetian Scene*, *c.*1840–45; 31¼ × 31; Tate Gallery

505. (Cat. 532) *A River seen from a Hill*, *c.*1840–45;
31 × 31¼; Tate Gallery

506. (Cat. 505)
Procession of Boats with Distant Smoke, Venice, *c.*1845;
$35\frac{1}{2} \times 47\frac{1}{2}$; Tate Gallery

507. (Cat. 506)
Festive Lagoon Scene, Venice, c.1845; $35\frac{3}{4} \times 47\frac{3}{4}$; Tate Gallery

508. (Cat. 507) *Riva degli Schiavone, Venice: Water Fete*, *c.*1845; $28\frac{3}{8} \times 44\frac{1}{4}$; Tate Gallery

509. (Cat. 508) *Venetian Festival*, *c.*1845; $28\frac{1}{2} \times 44\frac{5}{8}$; Tate Gallery

510. (Cat. 501)
Venice, the Piazetta with the Ceremony of the Doge marrying the Sea, *c*.1835; 36 × 48; Tate Gallery

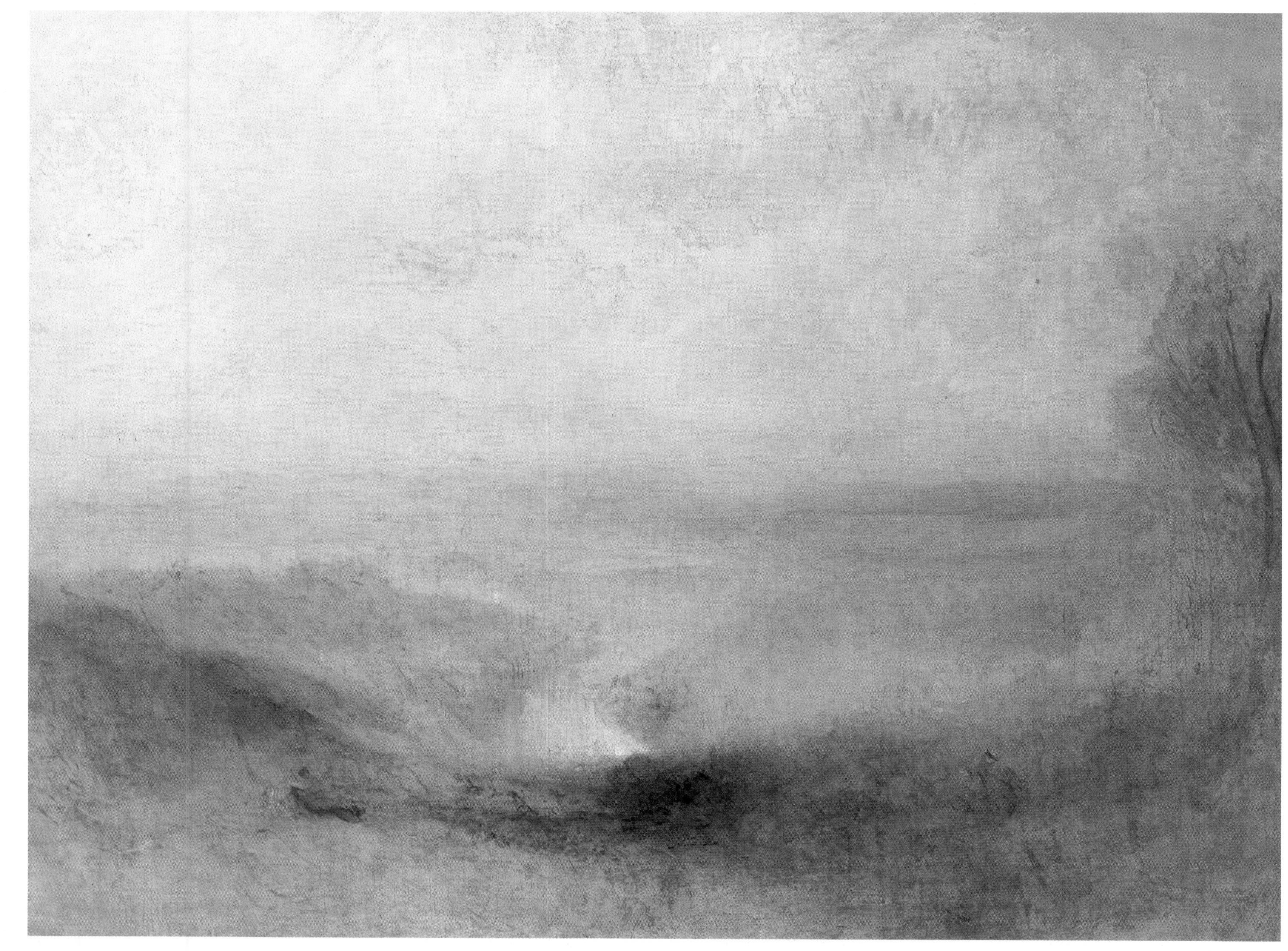

511. (Cat. 509) *Landscape with a River and a Bay in the Distance*, *c.*1840–50; 37 × 48½; Musée du Louvre, Paris

512. (Cat. 510) *The Falls of the Clyde*, *c.*1840–50; 35 × 47; the Trustees of the Lady Lever Art Gallery, Port Sunlight

513. (Cat. 511)
Landscape with Walton Bridges, *c.*1840–50; $34 \times 46\frac{1}{4}$; Estate of the late Mr H. S. Morgan, New York

514. (Cat. 512) *Norham Castle, Sunrise*, *c.*1840–50; $35\frac{3}{4} \times 48$; Tate Gallery

515. (Cat. 513)
Landscape: Woman with Tambourine,
c.1840–50; $34\frac{3}{4} \times 46\frac{1}{2}$;
Mrs M. D. Fergusson

516. (Cat. 514)
Europa and the Bull,
*c.*1840–50; $35\frac{7}{8} \times 47\frac{7}{8}$;
Taft Museum,
Cincinnati, Ohio

517. (Cat. 515) *Sunrise, a Castle in a Bay: 'Solitude'*, *c.*1840–50; $35\frac{3}{4} \times 48$; Tate Gallery

518. (Cat. 516)
Sunrise, with a Boat between Headlands, *c.*1840–50; 36 × 48; Tate Gallery

519. (Cat. 517) *Landscape with River and Distant Mountains*, *c.*1840–50; $36\frac{1}{4} \times 48\frac{1}{4}$; Walker Art Gallery, Liverpool

520. (Cat. 518) *The Ponte delle Torri, Spoleto*, *c.*1840–50; 36 × 48; Tate Gallery

521. (Cat. 519) *Inverary Pier, Loch Fyne: Morning*, *c.*1840–50; 36 × 48; Yale Center for British Art, Paul Mellon Collection

522. (Cat. 521) *Mountain Scene with Lake and Hut*, *c.*1840–45; Tate Gallery

523. (Cat. 522)
Mountain Landscape,
*c.*1840–45; 28 × 38;
Tate Gallery

524. (Cat. 520) *The Val d'Aosta*, *c.*1840–50; 36 × 48; National Gallery of Victoria, Melbourne

525. (Cat. 523) *The Thames above Waterloo Bridge*, *c.*1830–35; $35\frac{5}{8} \times 47\frac{5}{8}$; Tate Gallery

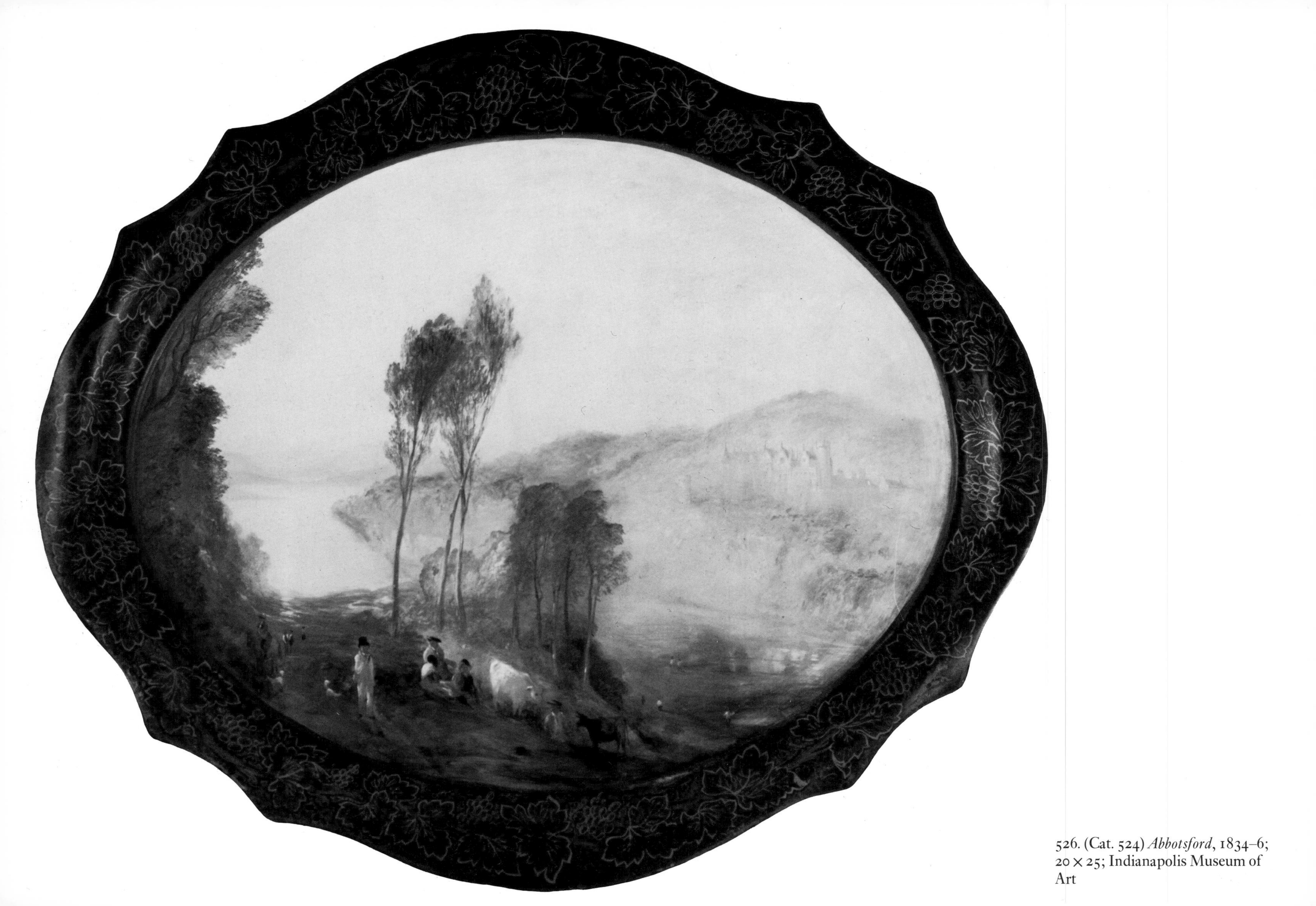

526. (Cat. 524) *Abbotsford*, 1834–6; 20 × 25; Indianapolis Museum of Art

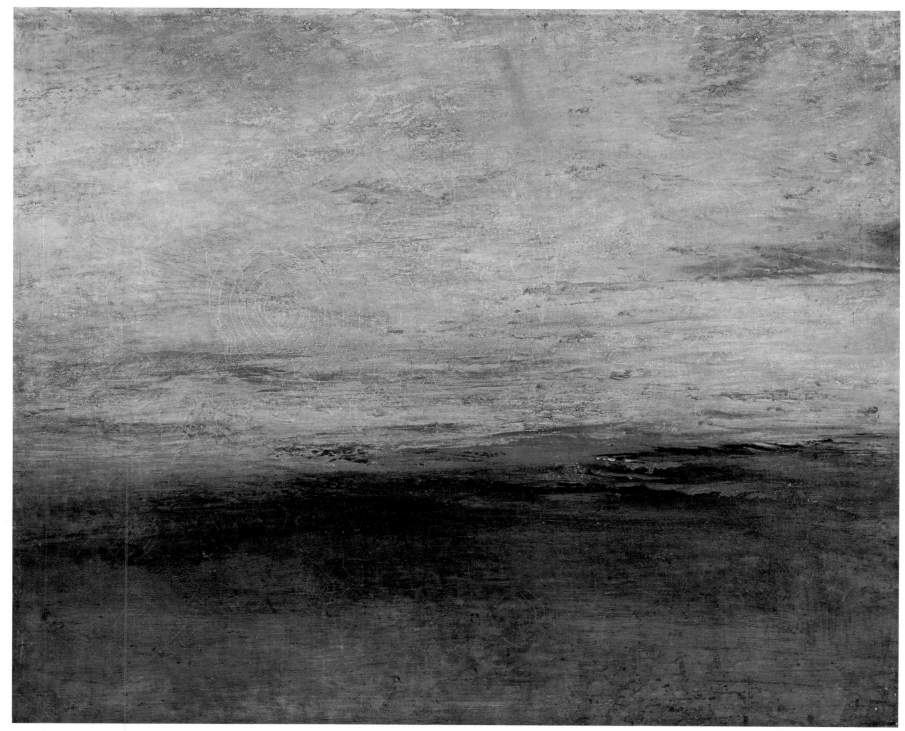

527. (Cat. 525) *Sunset*, *c.*1830–35?; $26\frac{1}{4} \times 32\frac{1}{4}$; Tate Gallery

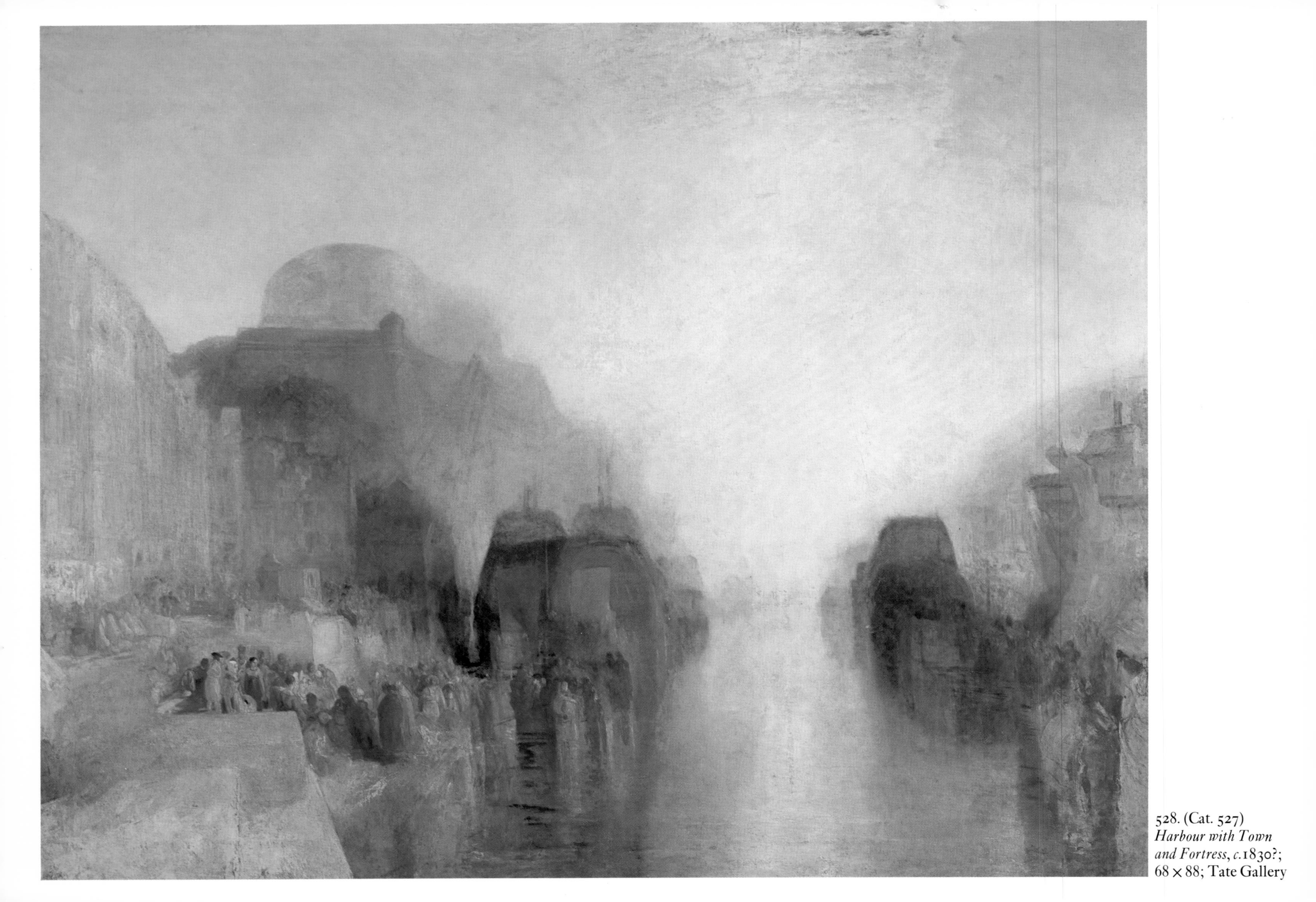

528. (Cat. 527)
Harbour with Town and Fortress, *c.*1830?; 68 × 88; Tate Gallery

529. (Cat. 528) *Estuary with Rocks and Buildings*, *c.*1830–40; $68 \times 95\frac{3}{4}$; Tate Gallery

530. (Cat. 529) *Seaport in the Grand Style*, *c.*1830–40?; $68 \times 95\frac{3}{4}$; Tate Gallery

531. (Cat. 530) *Extensive Landscape with River or Estuary and a Distant Mountain*, *c.*1830–40?; $55\frac{1}{2} \times 99$; Tate Gallery

532. (Cat. 531) *Landscape with Water*, *c.*1840–45; 48 × 71¾; Tate Gallery

533. (Cat. 544) British School, Nineteenth Century, *A Fresh Breeze, Part Copy of 'Sheerness and the Isle of Sheppey'*; $15\frac{1}{2} \times 19$; Tate Gallery

534. (Cat. 542) Sir Augustus Wall Callcott, *Copy of 'Sheerness and the Isle of Sheppey'*, *c.*1807–8; $27\frac{1}{2} \times 35\frac{1}{4}$; Tate Gallery

535. (Cat. 543) Sir Augustus Wall Callcott *Copy of 'Sheerness and the Isle of Sheppey'*, *c.*1807–8; $14\frac{1}{8} \times 18$; Ashmolean Museum, Oxford

536. (Cat. 548) Sir Joshua Reynolds or his Studio, *Portrait of a Lady*; $29\frac{3}{4} \times 24\frac{1}{2}$; Tate Gallery

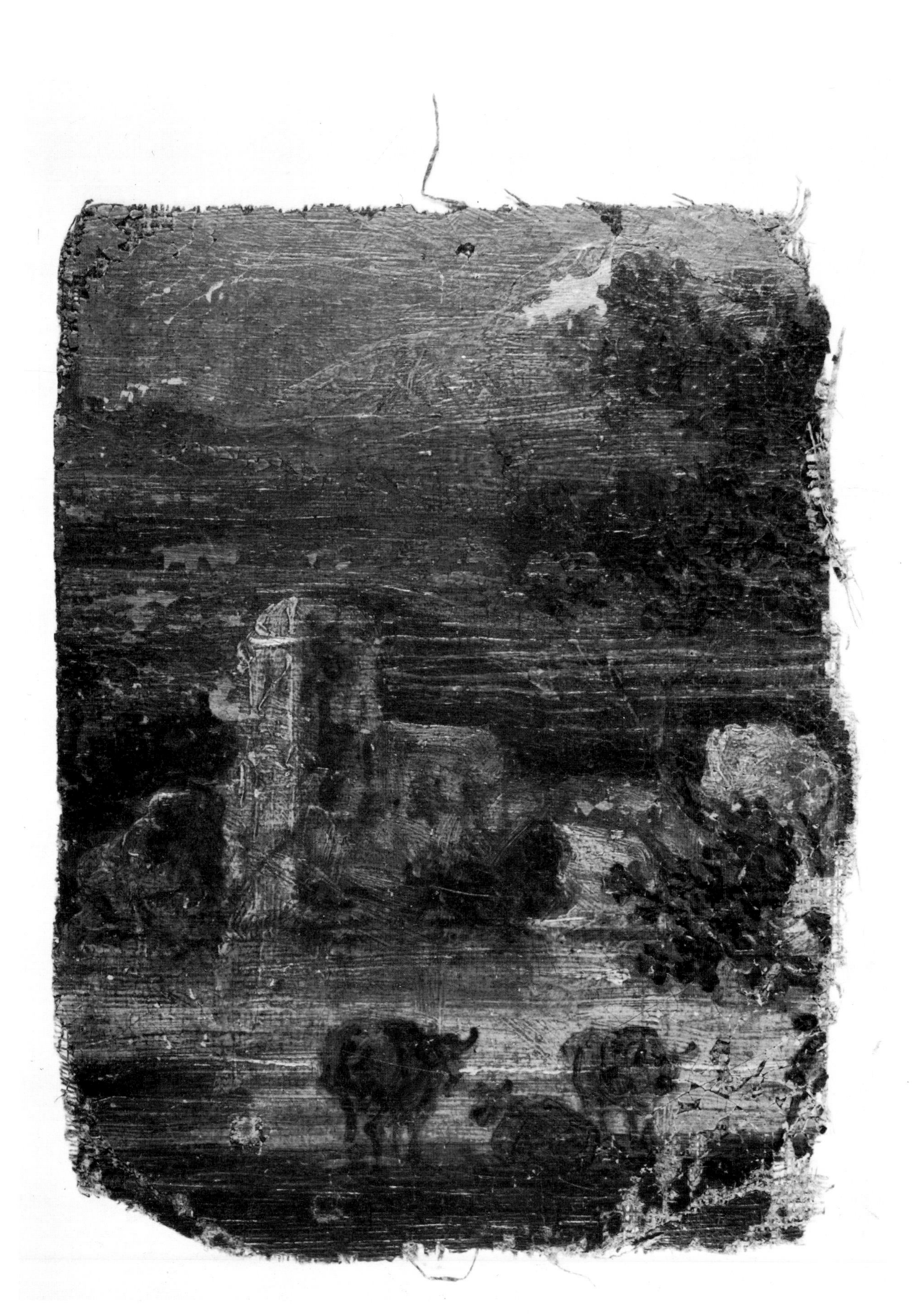

537. (Cat. 547a) Richard Wilson or his Studio, *Ruined Church beside a River, with Castle in the Foreground*; 8 × 6; British Museum

538. (Cat. 545) Richard Wilson or his Studio, *Tivoli: the Cascatelle*; 29 × 38; Tate Gallery

539. (Cat. 546) Richard Wilson or his Studio, *Valley with a Bridge over a River*; $39\frac{3}{4} \times 53\frac{3}{4}$; Tate Gallery

540. (Cat. 547)
Richard Wilson or
his Studio,
Niagara Falls;
$39\frac{1}{2} \times 53\frac{3}{4}$; Tate
Gallery

541. (Cat. 549) Formerly attributed to Turner, *Bath Abbey: West Front*; 42 × 50; present whereabouts unknown

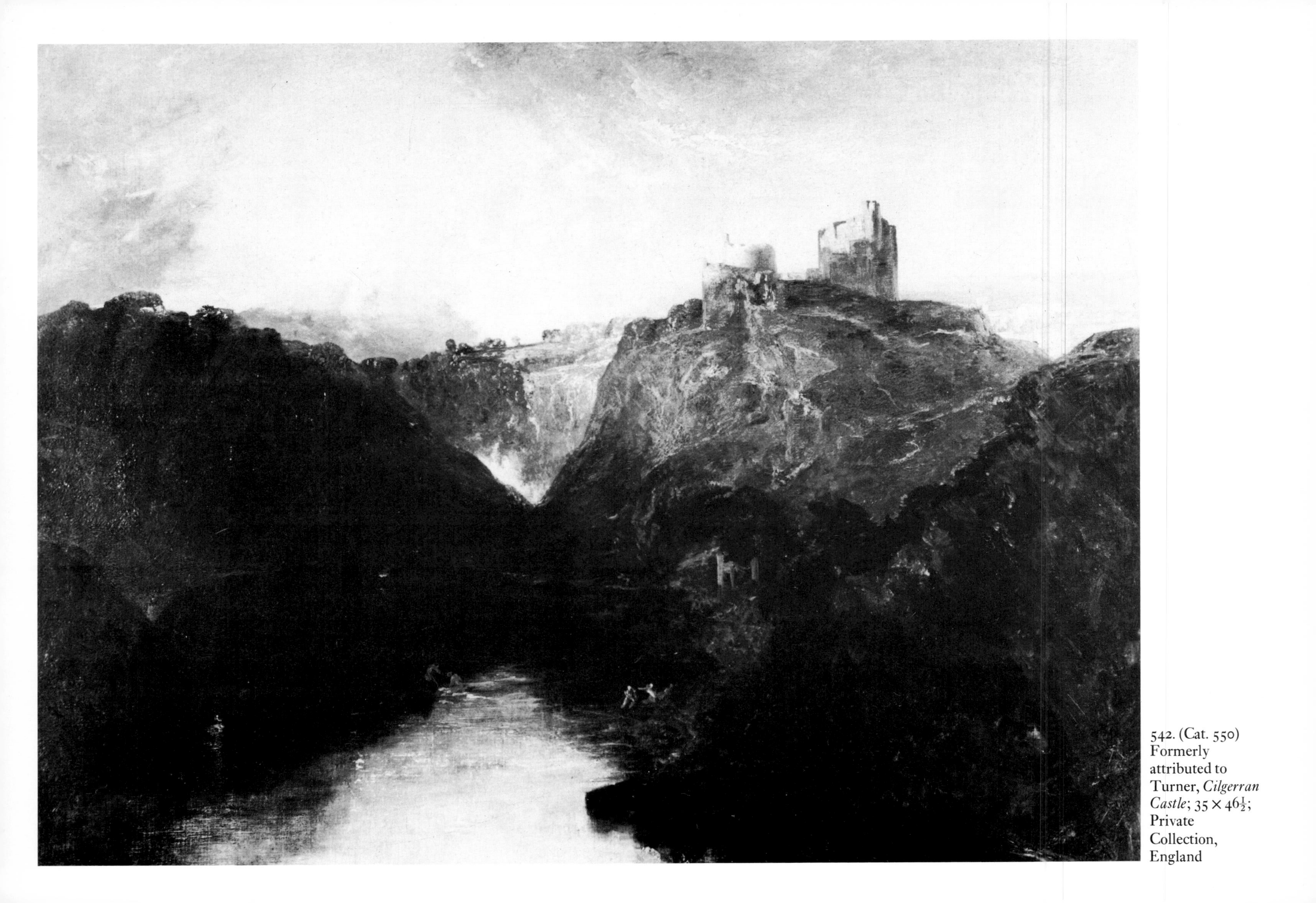

542. (Cat. 550) Formerly attributed to Turner, *Cilgerran Castle*; 35 × 46½; Private Collection, England

543. (Cat. 551a)
Landscape with Distant Church;
$8\frac{7}{16} \times 10\frac{1}{2}$; British Museum

544. (Cat. 552)
Formerly attributed
to Turner, *The Fight
on the Bridge*;
$17 \times 23\frac{3}{4}$; Royal
Albert Memorial
Museum and Art
Gallery, Exeter

545. (Cat. 553) Formerly attributed to Turner, *Old London Bridge*; $40\frac{1}{8} \times 49\frac{1}{2}$; Taft Museum, Cincinnati, Ohio

546. (Cat. 554) Formerly attributed to Turner, *Edinburgh and Calton Hill from St. Anthony's Chapel*; $33\frac{1}{4} \times 44$; Henry E. Huntington Library and Art Gallery, San Marino

547. (Cat. 559) (*below*) Formerly attributed to Turner, *Caernarvon Castle*; 38×55; Museu du Arte de São Paulo

548. (Cat. 551) Formerly attributed to Turner, *A Stream between High Banks*; $17\frac{3}{8} \times 12\frac{3}{4}$; Harris Museum and Art Gallery, Preston

549. (Cat. 557) Formerly attributed to Turner, *Margate Jetty*; 15 × 11; National Museum of Wales

550. (Cat. 555) Formerly attributed to Turner, *Off Margate*; $11\frac{1}{2} \times 17\frac{1}{2}$; National Museum of Wales

551. (Cat. 556) Formerly attributed to Turner, *Emigrants embarking at Margate*, $17\frac{1}{16} \times 21\frac{1}{16}$; Walker Art Gallery, Liverpool

552. (Cat. 556a) *The Phantom Ship*; 18 × 24; Whitworth Art Gallery, University of Manchester

553. (Cat. 558) Formerly attributed to Turner, *The Shipwreck*; 46 × 56¼; National Gallery of Canada, Ottawa

554. Sir Augustus Wall Callcott after Turner, *Fishermen becalmed previous to a Storm, Twilight*, 1799 (see Cat. 8)

555. After Turner, *Calm*, plate 44 from the *Liber Studiorum*, published April 1812; $7 \times 10\frac{1}{2}$ (see Cat. 8, 93 and 94)

556. Study for *The Army of the Medes (?)*, exh. 1801; $5\frac{1}{4} \times 7\frac{3}{4}$; British Museum, 'Dinevor' sketchbook, XL, pp.58 verso and 59 (see Cat. 15)

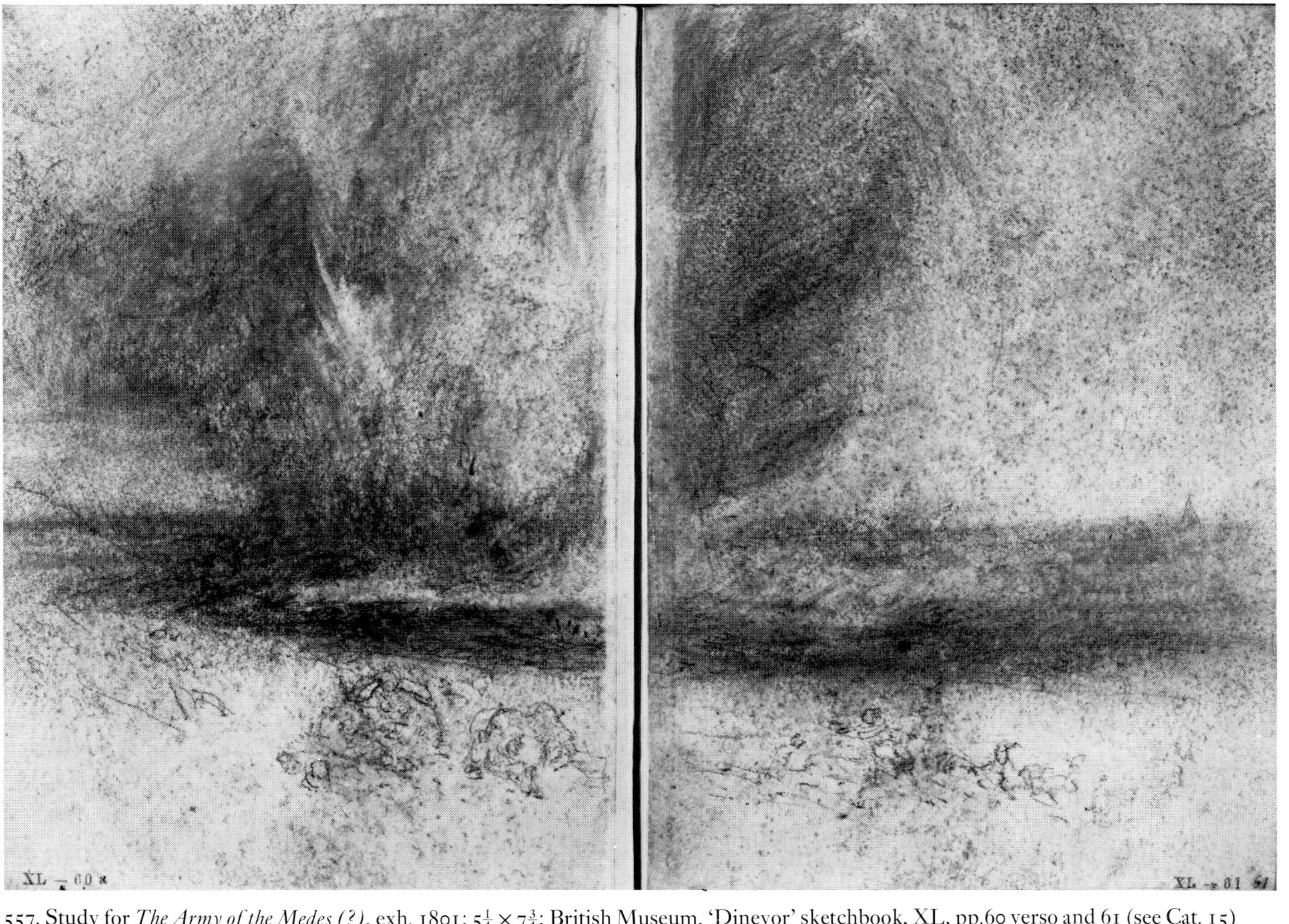

557. Study for *The Army of the Medes (?)*, exh. 1801; $5\frac{1}{4} \times 7\frac{3}{4}$; British Museum, 'Dinevor' sketchbook, XL, pp.60 verso and 61 (see Cat. 15)

558. Study for *The Army of the Medes (?)*, exh. 1801; $10\frac{3}{4} \times 17\frac{1}{8}$; British Museum, 'Calais Pier' sketchbook, LXXXI, p.165 (see Cat. 15)

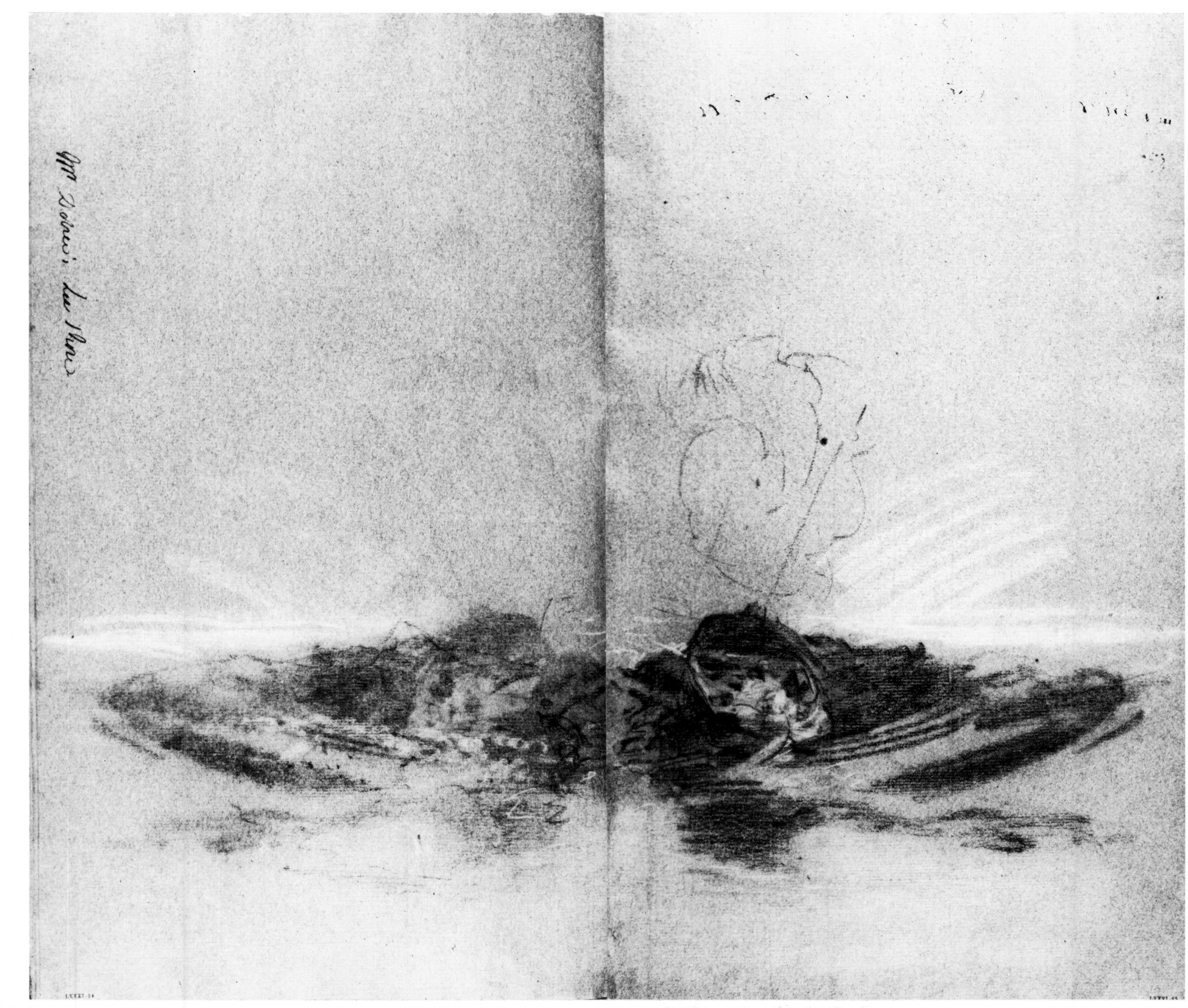

559. Study for *Fishermen upon a Lee-Shore*, exh. 1802; $17\frac{1}{8} \times 21\frac{1}{2}$; British Museum, 'Calais Pier' sketchbook, LXXXI, pp.84 and 85 (see Cat. 16)

560. After Turner, *Rispah*, plate 46 from the *Liber Studiorum*, published April 1812; $7\frac{1}{16} \times 10\frac{3}{8}$ (see Cat. 79)

561. Reverse of *Steamer and Lightship*; Cat 279

562. Detail of inscription from *Forum Romanum*; Cat. 233

563. Detail of inscription from *Seascape with Distant Coast*; Cat. 467

a. Cat. 150, *c.*1803–5 (Plate 49)

b. Cat. 149, *c.*1804–6 (Plate 156)

c. Cat. 58, 1806–8 (Plate 68)

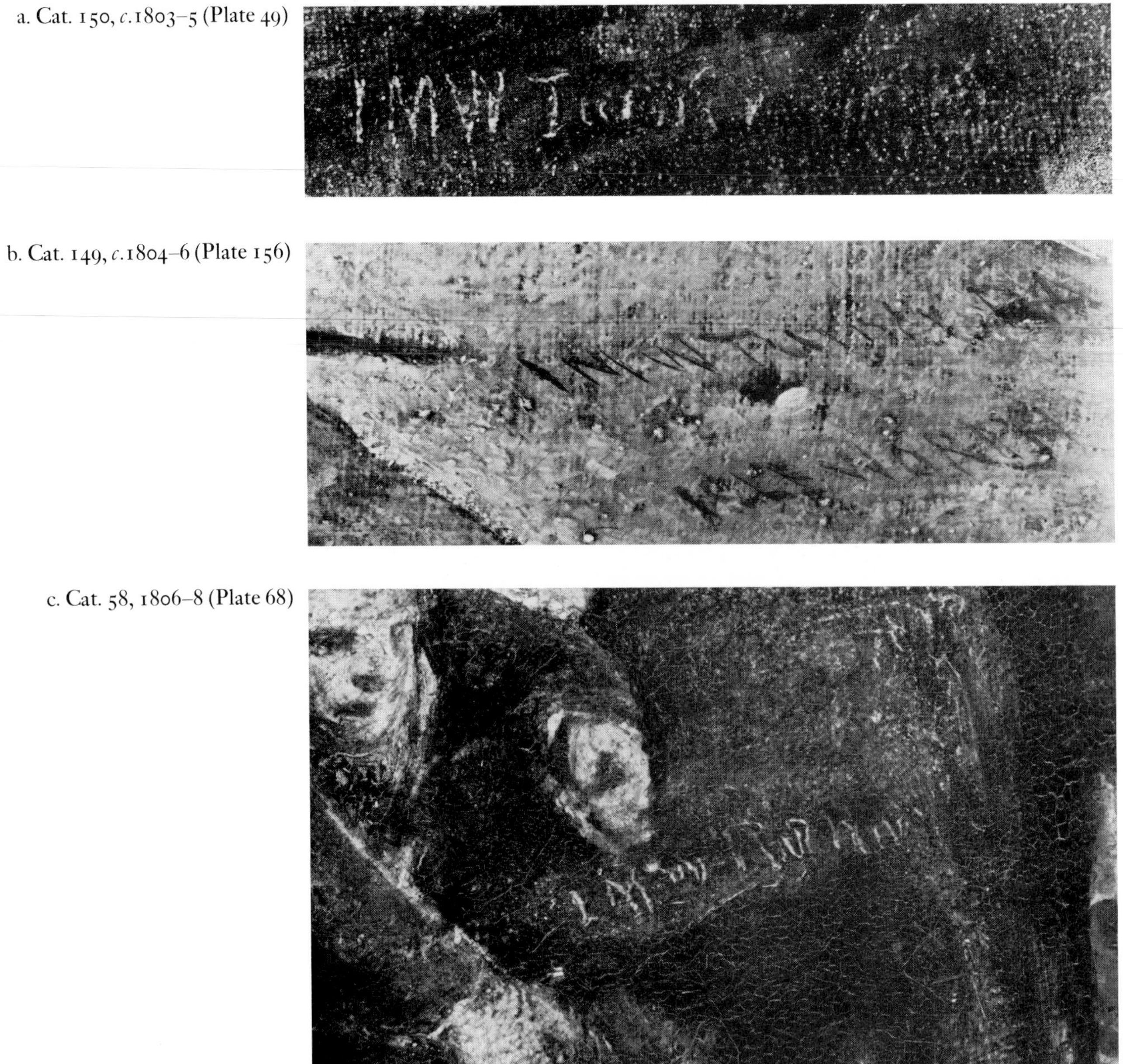

d. Cat. 72, 1808 (Plate 82)

e. Cat. 91, 1809 (Plate 101)

564. Turner's Signature

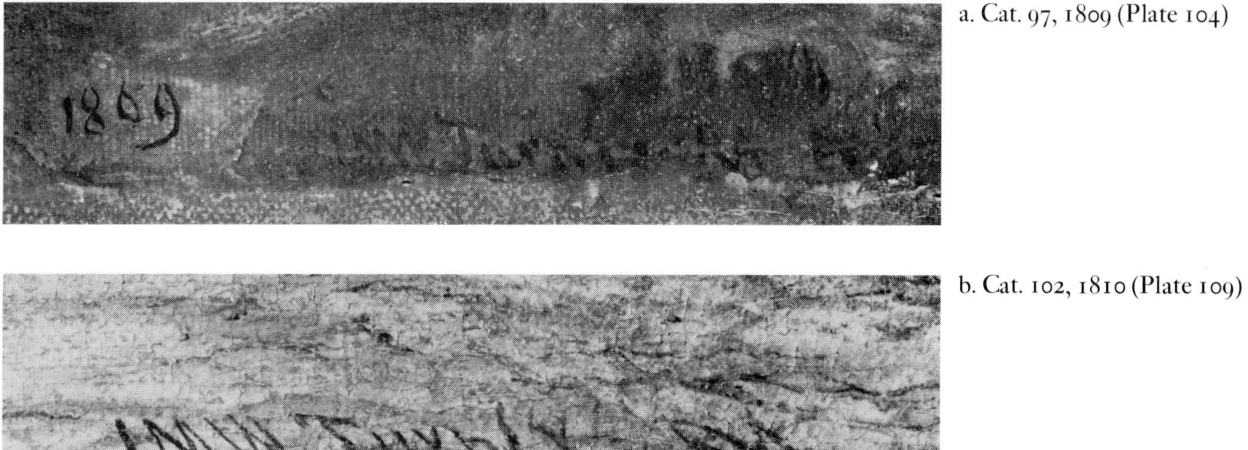

a. Cat. 97, 1809 (Plate 104)

b. Cat. 102, 1810 (Plate 109)

c. Cat. 137, 1818 (Plate 140)

d. Cat. 347, 1832 (Plate 350)

e. Cat. 403, 1843 (Plate 409)

566. Willem van de Velde, the Younger, *A Rising Gale*, 51 × 74½; Toledo Museum of Art, Toledo, Ohio (see Cat. 14)

567. Claude, *Jacob with Laban and his Daughters*; $56\frac{1}{2} \times 99$; Petworth House (see Cat. 128)

568. Titian, *The Martyrdom of St Peter*, engraved by Martino Rota; British Museum, London (see Cat. 150)

569. Van Dyck, *The Ninth Earl of Northumberland*; 54 × 47; Petworth House (see Cat. 338)

570. Van Dyck, *Lucy Percy, Countess of Carlisle*; $53\frac{1}{2} \times 43$; Petworth House (see Cat. 338 and 444)

571. Van Dyck, *Ann Carr, Countess of Bedford*; $53\frac{1}{2} \times 42\frac{1}{2}$; Petworth House (see Cat. 338 and 444)

572. George Jones, *The Burning Fiery Furnace*; $35\frac{1}{2} \times 27\frac{1}{2}$; Tate Gallery (see Cat. 346)